MW01587495

Two boys in a boat

Plus 563 Very Nice People

All the photos shown in this book can be viewed in high resolution colour at

www.facebook.com/two.boys.in.a.boat

You can send a message to us there as well

Copyright © 2013 Nick Mason, Sebastian Page Franklin, Steph Mason

All rights reserved

ISBN-13: 978-1492847984
ISBN-10: 149 284 7984

For our families

without whom we would probably still be
sitting on the couch
... dreaming

Diane Franklin, Peter Mason,
Steph Mason, Christopher Mason,
Alice Page Franklin and Alice Mason

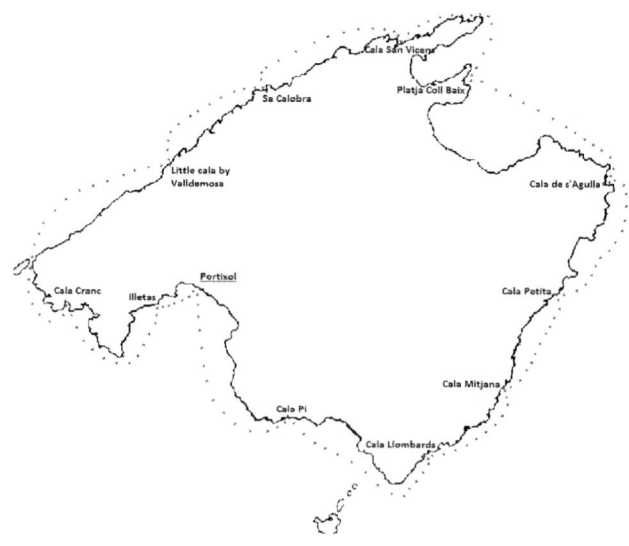

How it started

Seb: I was born in Palma de Mallorca in the summer of 1996. After my Mum had spent an hour recovering at the midwife's house, I was taken home to meet my sister, who promptly decided I was her doll.

"Home" was a 12 metre steel ketch moored in the Real Club Nautico, and a few hours after my arrival, Mum and Dad's friends, Pete and Steph Mason, came round to view me. Pete and Steph also lived on a sailing boat with their children. The Dads often worked on boats together and they'd become close friends.

With my arrival the group of kids was: Chris Mason – almost three; Alice Page – two; Alice Mason – six months; and me, Sebastian. Because there were two Alices, my sister became known as "Big Alice" while Alice Mason was "Little Alice". This has stuck even though "Little Alice" is now a head taller than "Big Alice".

With the arrival of Nick, eighteen months after me, the Masons reluctantly abandoned their life afloat and bought a dilapidated house with a jungle behind it which we all helped to clear in return for vast Sunday lunches. Even at that stage, Pete could whip his miniature crew into an organised team of weeders, diggers or dry stone wall builders. Slowly ancient trees were uncovered and terrace by terrace the garden began to emerge.

With the Masons on land, we were the Warriors! The last of the live aboard families still afloat in Palma. In the summer we would sail to Menorca or further afield, dropping our anchor in deserted bays, swimming in crystal clear waters, walking along sands with no other footprints but our own.

When we returned there would be a wistful longing in Pete and Steph's eyes as they heard of the latest travels from my parents.

Dad and Pete were working on the same boat together when the film *Titanic* came out on VHS. Although the Masons' lounge was tiny and only boasted two chairs, Mum and Steph sat resplendent in feather boas while Dad and Pete sported lifebelts, as the four of them spent the evening totally reliving the story while the five of us were tucked up on li-los in the next room.

When Dad suddenly died just before Christmas 2000 we had no option but to come ashore. At the time I was four and my sister was six; most people would have run for the safety nets available to widows in the UK, to the comfort of family, and the ease of life speaking your native language. Mum didn't.

She sold the boat, found a house and got a job in the nautical industry. She was quickly promoted and we changed schools to La Immaculada where Chris, Alice and Nick already studied. The school is in Palma's El Terreno district which is a few minutes' walk from the Masons' house. Every day we would race up the hill ready for a huge lunch and brief siesta before the afternoon school session. When Mum had to travel to boat shows or other nautical meetings abroad, we just moved into the Masons' house, and once we were teenagers, my sister and I had keys to the house just the same as Chris, Alice and Nick.

Somehow Mum managed to keep us in Mallorca and ensure we still went sailing, canoeing, windsurfing and diving. The five of us might not have had state-of-the-art equipment, but it never stopped us from doing anything we wanted to.

Although I was in the same class at school as

Little Alice, I've always had a lot in common with Nick. Like me, he loves all animals, except cockroaches, and admits to having been responsible for the adoption of at least nine of the current animal count at the Mason house. He joined the same stables as me in Calvia and ended up riding the same horse I had won the Infanta Elena Trophy on some years before. If we're chilling we'll both choose a David Attenborough programme or something like *Whale Wars*.

The last time we were all having dinner together Steph got us to go round the table and say a word that described each person for us. This was the result:

Diane
Mama 2 (from Chris)
Extremely reliable
Lovable but strict
Genuinely good person
Professional
Over protective
Survivor

Steph
Hugs
Friendship
Generous
Another Mummy (from Seb)
Huggable
Good friend
Understanding

Pete
The Captain
Totally reliable

Helpful
F***ing Aries
A rock
Funny
Cheeky

Chris
Musical
Loving
Poet
Passionate
Layered
Complex
Kind

Big Alice
Smiley
Spiritual
Outgoing
Caring
Happy
Creative
High on life

Little Alice
Bubbly
Full of life
Kind
Crazy
Hyper
Free
Spontaneous

Seb
Ladies' Man
Sensitive
Reliable
Wise
Responsible
Thoughtful
A friendly face

Nick
Laughs
Positive
Intelligent
Very kind
Talkative
Loving
Smart Arse

I guess that must be fairly accurate as the eight of us know each other better than anyone else on the island.

So, to sum up, Mum worked, while having a worrying ability to always know if we hadn't done our homework; Steph fed us, and taught us English so we wouldn't be totally illiterate in our parental tongue; and Pete got us to shoot air rifles and build hen houses while the years slid by, until …

Nick: I was lying in the garden pretending to revise and supervising Thumper's free hop to make sure he didn't get too adventurous and end up as next door's dog's dinner. (Dad says I should explain that Thumper is a rabbit, although I reckoned the name, plus the activity of "hopping" had his species covered. However, as he pointed out, we were once given a kitten called "Bunny", proving that confusing names happen in animals as well as celebrity kids. So, to be clear, Thumper is a large, white, lop-eared rabbit that was abandoned at the local vets and found his way into our "zoo" a few hours later, after the veterinary nurse gave me the doe-eyed-treatment and a few words about the Son Reus pet pound. I promptly relayed this to Mum, embellished with a snivel, which had predictable results. Thumper is very affectionate and house trained, but has an unfortunate fetish of chewing on electrical cables which, incredibly, hasn't cost him his life, although it may have shortened Dad's.)

Anyway, to get back to my revision, I had arranged an impressive number of textbooks around me, although none of them seemed to be impregnating any of their information into my brain, so, when Thumper fell asleep underneath the lemon verbena bush I rolled onto my back and stared at an endless expanse of sky. Occasional aircraft trails slowly faded into scattered white dots, as the odd cloud moved across my arc of vision. This is what summer will be like, I told myself, while finding it quite easy to omit the sentence Mum would have added of: "... only if you pass all your exams first!"

Life's so much better when you mute the sound on all the reasonable things you know your parents would say.

I pictured myself at the very start of the summer holidays; being able to get up late, having nothing I *had* to do, drifting off in our little dinghy, Rocky, whenever the whim grabbed me.

It grabbed me. I was floating around, sailing

gently, a horizon filled with flat calm water, and me.

Only me? That wouldn't work. I'm not a loner.

I put Chris in the boat. In my imagination he instantly took over as Captain and I could feel myself getting annoyed with him. I was losing my own chilled vision. I swapped him for Alice. That wasn't convincing either, she takes *so* long to get ready for anything we'd have never got this far! Overboard she went, as Seb appeared in the boat. Perfect …

…but after mentally sailing around a bit we arrived at the late afternoon; we were pulling Rocky back up the lethal glacial slipway, hauling on her covers, cycling home. It was a brutally active end to my awesome day, and I still had the whole summer in front of me.

I needed a different ending: we turned around and headed back through the waves until we arrived at a deserted beach. Miraculously we had both brought the hammocks we'd been given several Christmases ago but never used because the trees were never the right distance apart to put them up. But here, of course, the trees were perfect! We were swaying in our hammocks, I was strumming my guitar which, by a further miracle, had been in the boat yet had taken up absolutely no room. We were watching the sun go down with Rocky pulled up on the beach, deeply content that there was another blissful day to wake up to, and then another, and another. Total freedom.

That was it! We could spend the summer sailing round the island. I knew Seb would be up for it.

I rolled back onto my stomach, the text books were still there. No time for them … I needed a strategy. Mum and Dad might make noises about my age or competence, but they'd be more lenient with Seb.

Maybe his Mum would be the same towards me and we could each work on playing to the opposite parental soft spots.

We needed to present the idea as if we couldn't possibly imagine them saying "No". We could make it the lazy Mediterranean equivalent of a Masai warrior trekking his first lion, or an Aborigine going Walkabout. Perhaps we could edge the idea into the conversation one dinner time and then make them believe they had actually agreed to it.

I reached out for my phone to text Seb: "Do you want to sail Rocky round Mallorca with me this summer?"

It was time to stack my books and droop Thumper round my neck. As I walked back to the house I felt as if I'd had a massively productive afternoon. Surely, if we were allowed to go, I might be able to stop dreaming and study really hard – yes, that was another argument I could use, if I needed to!

We've been messing around together for a while!

Seb: "Of course!" I texted back. As if he needed to ask! The idea made my bus ride home fly past, but by the time I arrived in Calvia I had discovered several mountains that would need to be tackled before we stood a chance of getting out to sea.

The first was how to convince my Mum and sister that escaping with Nick was sufficiently important to absolve me from all my normal chores. If we were talking about a few days, I could probably barter, but Nick's plan involved far more freedom than that.

This required careful preparation. I needed something that would appeal to their better natures; something big enough to make them overlook the terrace sweepings, dishwasher unloadings and morning dog walkings I was intending to dump on them.

"Call me when u can, I've had a great idea!" was my next text to Nick. We could do the sail in order to collect money for charity.

Mum had always harboured dreams of working for a charity, and my sister had worked as a volunteer at some of the food centres around Palma that sprang up during Spain's financial crisis. Little Alice had also done a couple of stints at a food centre in the middle of the island. Part of the produce handed out at the food centres comes via volunteers who offer to gather up the oranges and lemons that many people with rural properties just allow to drop and rot on the ground. These are then distributed among poor families to ensure they get fresh fruit and vitamin C. All of these projects are run by the charity Mediterranea which was the brainchild of our doctor, Michael Stoma.

Mediterranea (www.mediterraeaong.com)

operates a multitude of different programmes in Africa and, since the need became evident closer to home, in Mallorca too. They attempt to help wherever they see genuine hardship and every euro that is donated goes in its entirety to the projects as there are no paid workers. They've built schools and orphanages in Ethiopia, helped provide school books for less wealthy families on the island, and are currently developing a scheme here to ensure every primary school child gets daily milk through a system similar to the one our parents remember operating in Britain when they were young.

Dr. Stoma is hot on nutrition and makes no secret of the fact that he believes McDonalds should carry a government health warning which should be as strongly worded as those on cigarette packets. It's all part of his passion to get the message across that preventative "medicine" begins in earliest childhood and that the effects of poor diet can be traced to chronic health problems in later life.

Seeing as Dr Stoma is also Nick's doctor, and last year the Masons had delivered some discarded reading glasses to people in Uganda for the charity, Mediterranea seemed a good place to start.

However, there was also a pull on my conscience towards Ondine (www.asociacionondine.org) , a marine conservation association run by super-cool Aussie, Brad Robinson, and his awesome Spanish wife, Bea.

Brad is a diver, and it was through the five of us doing PADI courses that we had originally met. Brad also adores sharks.

While most people get excited about the health of our sea life through images of smiling dolphins and majestic whales, Brad's vision is of Great Whites. He's so enamoured by them that it's an absolute certainty, within twenty minutes of meeting him, he will have convinced you that Jaws is your dearest friend.

It's all about healthy food chains. There's no way I could ever present the shark propaganda with his flare, but the nuts and bolts are, if the animals at the top of the food chain are abundant then you know everything beneath them is OK.

With the current absence of Great Whites around Mallorca – the last one was caught off Pollensa in the 1970s – Brad is striving, through Asociación Ondine, to make many more people aware of the island's marine reserves, tackle the problems of sea rubbish and sustainable fishing, and track the breeding patterns of stingrays and other species that could begin to kick start a return to teeming life within our seas.

With these two programmes already part of our families' lives, we could definitely find a "cause" to sail for. This, I hoped, would soften parental responses to the number of sandwiches and bottles of sun block they would need to supply if we were to do the trip. However, there were still plenty of obstacles to be overcome.

Nick: "Seb and I want to sail Rocky round the island to raise money for Mediterranea this summer," I announced between mouthfuls of spaghetti bolognaise.

"Cool," Alice responded.

"Sleeping on the beaches each night?" Mum asked.

"Or at friends' houses … " I ventured to try and keep her on side, "between us we know people with houses in a lot of different areas."

"You'll need a proper training programme," she

continued.

"Of course!" I said.

"At least twenty hours before you leave …"

"Plus capsize and man-overboard practice," Dad added, already tapping his iphone to see how many miles there were in a circumnavigation. Mum was obviously distracted as she didn't murmur about his blatant example of dinner-table-Googling. She would usually have gone ballistic.

"It's 160 nautical miles," Dad announced, "should take you ten to fourteen days I reckon."

… Was that a "yes"? It sounded very like a "yes"! I braced myself for the list of "BUTS".

"You'll have to phone us every morning for a forecast," Mum began, "and if we say you're not to sail you can clean the beach or something, but you must NOT sail without speaking to us first."

"OK," that one didn't knock the shine of freedom off the project too much.

"You'll need to hug the coastline, no massive tacks out to sea, and wear life jackets at all times."

"Oh come on Mum! We can swim!"

"That's non-negotiable Nick!" I could see the sides of her mouth compressing; she was going to get hyper. "You only need to capsize and one of you be knocked out by the boom …"

"It will be summer, we'll boil in life jackets!" I argued.

"You get tiny ones now that are gas operated, we've got a load of them on the boat," Dad said, "they're more like harnesses."

"Perhaps we could get nautical companies to lend or donate things to us for the trip," I said slowly, "lots of people haven't got spare cash to sponsor with but they might be willing to help in other ways."

"That's a good idea, especially if you thank everyone who helps, so that they all feel part of your adventure," Mum said. It was a relief to see she'd been successfully deflected from the health and safety rant she'd been about to embark on.

"We could have a blog to let people know how things are going, and what things we still need, and to thank them when they give us stuff," I replied.

"With a link to Mediterranea's bank account," Chris added, "so people can sponsor direct."

"They'll also need sponsor sheets though," Alice said, "so we can get people at school involved."

This was sounding like an unwaverable "YES" to me, and in my happiness I even magnanimously allowed Chris to scrape out the last bit of spaghetti from the bowl without uttering a word.

"But none of this can detract from the time you need to spend on your exams," Mum began, "they have to be your focus. I don't deny it's a great idea and, if you're properly prepared, you should have a wonderful time, but exams come first! There's no doubt at all that if Seb's grades start slipping Diane will put a stop to this in a heartbeat, and the same goes for you."

"OK Mum"

"You have a revision plan already, so before you go any further you need to show me you're still keeping up with that, and also fitting in sailing practice," she was in full swing now. "If you really want to do this you'll have to give up TV watching for the next few months."

"Yes Mum."

There were plenty of BUTS being thrown about, yet by the time dessert was cleared away, sailing Rocky around Mallorca to raise money for Mediterranea had been absorbed into the family as a fact and I was attempting to mask my complete jubilation and contain my urge to race upstairs and ring Seb. As I had achieved a "Yes", I was terrified he might be receiving a "No", surely nothing could stop us now.

Seb: "What do Pete and Steph say?" Mum asked.

"They're all for it. Ring them if you don't believe me!"

"It's not that I don't believe you, but I want it to be very clear, your school work comes first and I'm sure they'll feel the same about Nick…"

My conversation was going much the same as the one Nick told me he had gone through. I had no doubt Mum would be on the phone within seconds of me leaving the room, but at least for now all three adults seemed to be on board.

Before the parents had too much of a chance to over-think things, we sent an email to Dr. Stoma to tell him of our idea and ask if we could meet up. The response was immediate, so the following Saturday afternoon Mum and I met Nick and Steph outside the surgery in Portals Nous. Dr. Stoma was great. The embodiment of enthusiasm, offering us any assistance we might need. He's accustomed to dealing with crew from the island's sizeable yachting community, so soon his mind was tripping over itself in an eager rampage towards ever larger projects.

"It's a fantastic idea! I'm sure we could get some of the large yachts involved … maybe get a fleet together … we have good connections with IB3 television if you think they might be helpful …"

I could feel Nick begin to sag as he perched on his

waiting room chair. Our vision was being swamped with a tidal wave of extra people. The panicky feeling that comes when a long anticipated treat is being inadvertently removed by someone genuinely kind, so you can't say anything, was rising through my chest as I struggled to form a convincing argument against the Doctor's expanding plans. More boats would definitely raise more money, so how could I complain without making it sound as if fund raising was some kind of ruse?

"Perhaps it could grow into an annual event with a fleet of boats, but I think there's a danger of destroying the purity of the idea, and the experience for the boys, if other boats were involved this year."

Steph had said what I wanted to, and Mum was backing her up. That brief moment, when I thought we were going to have our solo adventure philanthropically bulldozed away from us, had made the dream more precious than ever.

At once Dr. Stoma understood, and it was all OK. The roles had been put back to "adventure and freedom" first, "amount raised for charity" important, but still second.

"I walked round the coast of Mallorca with a friend at your age," Dr. Stoma said, becoming nostalgic. "We met a group of Swedish students camping in a bay one night … it was magical. Everyone needs a journey like that." And then we were looking at calendars and the dates of the end of the school year, Nick's work experience commitments and my trip to Menorca for the Sant Juan fiestas.

"It looks like Saturday the 6th of July is the first possible start date," Mum said, as the others noted it down.

"Before we start looking for sponsors and posting a blog we'll need to talk to Brad and Bea," Nick said as we left the surgery, having promised to keep in touch with Dr. Stoma throughout the next couple of months, and clutching some Mediterranea stickers to put on Rocky.

"I'm at the Crew Show next week, and Ondine have a stand there too, so find an afternoon when you both have some time after school and come along," Mum replied. It was all falling into place.

Still in our uniforms, Mum got the two of us into the Crew Show a few days later. She'd already spoken to a number of other nautical companies who were exhibiting there and they were all really positive and offering help.

"Legends!!!" Brad cried, as he saw us squeezing through the crowd. "What a great idea!" he said during a good couple of minutes of male back-slapping hugs. "We're already putting together a list of ways you can help with Ondine's research. It's going to be amazing!"

Nick and Seb with shark-mad-Brad

Nick: It didn't look "amazing" when we went down to Rocky that weekend. We had to go as we needed to have photos taken with the boat so we could start our blog. Mum had just completed a blogging course and was super keen to instruct us in the importance of "the visual" as well as "the written". However, "the visual" really wasn't looking great.

Wide grey puddles covered the boatyard and, for late April in Mallorca, we were uncharacteristically wrapped up in thick pullovers and anoraks. The wind was setting off a cacophony of slapping halyards with every gust, and the drizzle soon plastered our hair to our foreheads.

"It's more like sailing in Britain," Dad commented as we sloshed gallons of water out of Rocky's cover, which was adorned with a deep growth of green slime.

Inside the boat all the ropes were crisp with salt and age. The foot straps lay faded and frayed in a pool of brownish water while the laminates on the tiller had an unhealthy bulge. Screw heads that should have been stainless were rusted into place, and the black jamming cleats were brittle and bleached grey. The few stickers, put on by a long-forgotten owner, were cracked, pieces of them peeling and leaving streaks of brilliant white hull highlighted against the yellowing rest.

"It'll look better when the sun shines," I ventured with an uncertain grin at Seb.

"Only if you get on and do some maintenance," Dad said, as Mum leapt around like a demented leprechaun with her camera, "I'll take the tiller home now and put it in the vice. Reckon you're going to need some new ropes though."

Rocky wasn't in a sailable state, so it didn't really

matter that the weather was gross. We smiled on Mum's cue and stuck three of the Mediterranea stickers on the hull, which made the bad ones stand out even more. We did OK at putting one on either side of the bows but when Seb came to peel off the paper on the one for the stern it was slightly off horizontal – not sufficiently to look as if he'd meant to do it, just a crap job, so, of course, we had to let him know about it!

"Hey Dude, is that meant to be horizontal? I think you've totally lost man-points there."

"It's not that bad, is it?" he said stepping away from the abomination for a better look.

"No, you're right, if you tilt your head enough it's dead straight!"

We were thinking of encouraging local companies to put stickers on Rocky as an incentive to sponsor us or donate things we would need. We hoped Rocky would become colourful, and some of the dinks would be covered up, but we were either going to have to deliberately stick them on at weird angles, or get a hell of a lot better at judging what was "straight".

Arriving home with a lengthy to-do list, we began to get our first blog together, explaining who we were and what we wanted to do. I had read the book *Free Country* where two guys travelled from Lands' End to John O'Groats, starting off in just a pair of union jack underpants and asking for everything else they needed on the way. It was their quest to show what lovely people inhabit the British Isles. They managed to blag everything from clothes to food, beer and bicycles by having signs saying "I am officially a very nice person" for people who helped them to hold up when they took their photo. This gave me the idea of having a section on our blogs for Very Nice People and to make some signs of our own. *Free Country* is a great example of how helpful 99% of the population are and of the power of saying "thank you".

Finally, with the day's photos loaded onto the computer, it seemed as if we were ready to roll, and then we ran headlong into a brick wall.

We needed a name. Should it be in Spanish or English? Should it be serious or a bit jokey? Could we find something in Spanish that English people would also understand? Were there any undiscovered laws we were about to find out about the minute we published our intentions? Suddenly everyone had opinions but few had solutions. If we hadn't already spoken to Dr. Stoma and Brad the whole project might have been in danger of dying on a point of semantics.

After hours of wrangling, we settled on the name SailAid in a simple Calibri font in pale blue. It was the best of a bunch of ideas that nobody particularly liked. Then we used the descriptive line of "Two boys in a boat" on the English blog and "Dos jovenes y un barco" for the Spanish, and pressed "publish" on the first post with trembling fingers.

By the following morning a surprising number of people had sent us encouraging messages and a 16-year-old girl we'd never met had asked to join us in her boat. Things were looking up! We even had our first sponsor in the form of Canon Jim Hawthorne MBE, who was the priest who had christened me. He was about to pay one of his regular visits to the island and would leave money with us, which seemed a bit trusting, but then he didn't know what the boat was like.

Kay Halley from the Universal Bookshop in Portals Nous had sent an email to say how much she liked the idea and to offer us books for our journey.

"I'm not sure they'd survive, but thanks very much for the offer," I replied. "... you don't by any chance have a laminating machine, do you?" We would need to laminate the A4 charts we intended to make by cutting a big one up into chunks, plus our Very Nice Person signs.

"Yes!" came the answer, so, less than 24 hours after making the blog live and linking it to a Facebook page, with our chosen craft in an horrendous state and only suitable for sitting in on dry land, we had our first sponsor and our first offer of help from a local business.

I had a moment of blind panic that we were destined to end up looking completely idiotic to a horribly large number of people on a small island where everyone seems to know everything about everybody. What a bloody stupid thing to do!

Rocky: only fit for on land sailing!

Getting afloat

Seb: The spring of 2013 was exceptionally windy in Mallorca and after we had announced our grand plans we became exceedingly frustrated when, every time we wanted to get out on the water, there was a gale blowing. To look on the positive side, it did give us the opportunity to do some essential repairs and to renew the main halyard, which was dangerously thin in several places. Whilst we were re-threading it up the mast we sprayed liberal amounts of WD40 around the top wheel and used a screwdriver to bend out bits of the track where it nipped the sail edge.

A nautical web magazine, *Marina Live*, had contacted us and was promising to do an article, as was the Pollensa-based *Talk of the North* newspaper, which we were particularly pleased about because we knew very few people up there so we were hoping that a bit of publicity might mean people would recognise the boat and throw us the odd baguette.

Food was something Nick was particularly worried about, and its importance was growing in his mind as the state of the boat slowly improved. He's always been long, but in the past couple of years he's stretched far more than is natural and, with his head so far above the ground, he's liable to faint if not regularly stoked with sugar and carbohydrates. Mum and Steph have said they will send us off with a supply of tins but we will still need to buy things along the way and there are frequently no shops for miles around the small bays.

"I'll beg if necessary," Nick said when we discussed this thorny problem yet again. "I can make cute eyes," he claimed while performing an example, "and say 'I'm growing, please feed me!' that'll work."

"Either that, or you'll get taken into care before we get as far as Arenal," I replied. "I think we need to plan for your consumption levels and hope it doesn't sink Rocky!"

At last there was a Saturday without a hurricane, when we could get out on our first official training session.

We decided to launch Rocky from the slipway to the left of the main one because it looked as if the wind direction would make it easier to get out, even though it was situated between two pontoons full of moored boats. With both sails up and flapping, we anticipated making a couple of stylish tacks out, having smoothly fixed the rudder in place and got the centre plate down directly there was sufficient depth to do so. That was the plan.

Amid a jibing boom, lashing sheets and a rudder that completely refused to slot onto its pins, we careered from one side of the inlet to the other, bashing into various boats on the way as Nick attempted to do a Hawaii-canoe impression with our single paddle, which had almost no effect whatsoever except to fend off from other craft.

As it was the weekend there were plenty of people around to witness our embarrassment, and to save ourselves from even redder faces, Nick grabbed the painter and jumped over the side. As he swam us into deeper water, I was able to wiggle the rudder into place and sit at the helm attempting to look as if this was normal, while he towed Rocky passed an amused looking gentleman on one of the boats we had miraculously managed to avoid crashing into.

"Is that how it's meant to move?" the man asked as he bent over a couple of 150hp engines.

"It's easier than any other method at the moment," I replied as a blue-lipped Nick flopped back over the side.

"That was bloody freezing!" Nick chattered, his entire body looking like a puce plucked turkey, "we *have* got to get a second paddle."

As we put Rocky through her paces it was clear that a roll of sail tape might be pretty useful too, plus a few spare shackles and split pins because they had an uncanny ability to jump over the side when nobody was watching.

The substantial picnic we had brought was quickly reduced to two banana skins as the sea air, and the swim, made Nick even more ravenous than usual. We were intending to carry three-days' supply of food, but at this rate it would leave us no room for sleeping bags, tent or anything else that was vital.

By mid-afternoon we were knackered, but happy that we'd managed to get afloat and stay there for a reasonable amount of time. After putting Rocky to bed we cycled off to Palma Boat Show, for which Mum had given us a couple of free tickets. The sail had made us realise that we either needed to win the lottery – which both of us were too skint to play – or find some very, very nice people who would loan us things like modern lifejackets, a paddle and a substantial number of other bits. The Boat Show seemed a reasonable place to start.

In the end it wasn't particularly successful but at least we spoke to several nautical companies and came away with a couple more sponsors.

I left Nick at sixish and headed home as I was due to meet some friends in Magalluf later. That evening I was sitting in a bar, chilling with friends, when a seriously hot girl approached our table.

"Aren't you the SailAid boy?" she asked as my jaw hit the table and I could feel a soppy grin overtake my face.

"Yes!"

"Which one are you?" she continued as we all shuffled around to make room for her and her friends.

"Sebastian ..." I couldn't wait to hear Nick's reaction to this!

Leaving with the "substantial picnic" ...

Nick: "That's not cool. You should have called me. We're a team! ... You didn't even take photos ... You could have got me on speaker phone! Many things could have been done to make this better Dude!"

"There were a whole crowd of them ..." he said down the phone with some idea that this would be an excuse.

"How does that make it better?" I asked. "What nationality were they?"

"I don't know, they were speaking English but they weren't," he pretended to think before delivering the killer blow, "they were too blonde to be Spanish, and far too leggy!"

"Are you kidding me? They were all hot?" I could hear him doing a little dance down the phone.

While Seb had been experiencing film star treatment, I'd been having a pretty boring evening at home recounting the day's events to my parents.

"You could avoid all the flapping about by paddling out to a buoy and then putting up the sails," Mum commented.

"We just need to get better at it," I said wearily. Why couldn't she have faith that we'd be slick at it soon? "Anyway, in order to paddle out anywhere we need more than that one plastic paddle that looks as if it came off a kid's blow-up boat!"

"It probably did," Dad said. "Mum and I have been talking, we want to get you a PLB for the trip. You can take it in turns to strap it to your leg or something."

"PLB?"

"Personal Location Beacon, it's like an EPIRB but you set it off manually instead of it going off automatically when it's submerged, which would be no good for you two."

"Can't we ask a company to loan us one or something, we want to do this at the least cost possible," I said. It all sounded a bit major, it wasn't as if we were crossing the Atlantic.

"We want to be sure of getting a GPS one rather than the cheaper sort that has to triangulate your approximate position. If you do get into trouble we want Search and Rescue to be able to pin-point you. It's not as if it won't be used again, if any of you go climbing or trekking in the future you'll be able to take it with you."

"Before I forget," Mum chipped in, "Captain Kevin wants you to go and have breakfast with him in the Club de Mar bar tomorrow, ten-thirty."

So, while Seb was partying with girls who already thought he was some kind of hero, and sleeping-in late the next morning, I was watching a bad film at home and then getting up in time for toast with an 87-year-old who had recently had most of his vocal chords removed which meant I would need to be properly awake and concentrating if I was to understand our conversation – no wonder I was pissed off.

However, by the time I arrived at the bar in the morning I was feeling considerably happier. After all, if the Captain wanted to see me it had to mean he was intending to sponsor us, which was cool. Also, although I didn't know him well, my brother Chris had done quite a bit of work for Captain Kevin over the years and always said he was a good guy.

I found the Captain seated in his designated spot. He's been there so long that the Club have even put up a brass plaque with his name and undisputed right to the seat, in order to ensure that no unwary visitor usurps that particular piece of yellow vinyl cushion. From this throne, Captain Kevin O'Regan has spent more than 20 years banging the drum for his own pet charity, Joves Navegants, of which he is the Lifetime Patron.

Mum has been involved with Joves Navegants for almost as long as Captain Kevin, so both of them would have been delighted if we had chosen that organisation rather than Mediterranea. The charity teaches the island's most disadvantaged teenagers how to sail, and improves their social skills by taking them on trips where groups of them have to work together as a crew over an extended period. They are also taught about ecology, celestial navigation and boat maintenance. Anyone who shows interest is encouraged to study for qualifications to enable them to follow a career in local nautical industries.

With his full white beard and prodigious eyebrows, Captain Kevin is every inch the formidable Sea Dog, and as I approached I had a twinge that he might berate me for not collecting for Joves Navegants.

I couldn't have been more wrong! The moment I plonked myself opposite him, he leaned forward and growled, "Well, young Nick, how can I help?"

Losing his vocal chords has not made any difference at all to the Captain's ability to communicate – although Dad does say he sounds like a caricature of an axe-murderer on the phone. With or without a voice, the Captain was alive with ideas: he would get the bar to put one of our posters up, but we should produce a special one directing people who wanted more information to his chair; once there, he would ensure they signed away most of their worldly wealth to us; he would see if *Galaxie*, Joves Navegants' boat, was going down the North coast any time when we were off school so we could join the trip and take a look at the most challenging part of the circumnavigation before we arrived in Rocky; he would talk to the people in Joves Navegants about making up a SailAid fleet next year; there was no end to his energy.

"It's a wonderful thing to do, you'll never forget it. I did the same thing in 1942 when I was a nipper, round the coast of Ireland." He stared up at the ceiling remembering his epic voyage, "Seven hundred miles in a 14-foot, gaff-rigged wooden dinghy."

I was gobsmacked and could hardly imagine how much more preparation a trip like that would have taken. To get anywhere near the Captain's odyssey I calculated we'd need to sail round all the Balearic islands a couple of times each.

"Of course it was war time, but I was only arrested twice. The police thought I was a German spy," he laughed, "it didn't take long to prove I was Irish to the core though!"

By now I was in awe of this Master Mariner. It's incredible how easy it is to forget that old people have ever been my age, or to assume they've never done incredible things just because they've not come up in conversation.

I started asking Captain Kevin for any tips he could give us, realising I was in the presence of someone who had been there, done that and definitely got the T-shirt, and I shouldn't waste the opportunity to get as much information as possible out of him.

"Stick close to the shore where you're out of the way of U-boats and other big traffic," he cautioned, before wagging a sturdy index finger at me to emphasise his next point, "… and never, ever cleat-off your sheets when you're near cliffs as the down draughts can capsize you in a second. Always hold the sheets, then you'll automatically let go if you're hit by a blast. It could save you and the boat!"

Promising to send a bespoke poster and sponsor sheets with Chris when he came to give the Captain his computer lesson the next day, I left with the pledge of 100 euros if we made it all the way round, plus a new deep admiration for someone I'd known since I was born, but had suddenly realised I hadn't known anything about at all.

Nick with Captain Kevin O'Regan who sailed around Ireland in an open wooden dinghy during the latter part of World War Two ... and only got arrested twice! His sailing advice was worth its weight in gold, and he is a Very Nice Person!

Seb: Although it's great in one way, the amount of interest in SailAid is beginning to spook me. I've gone from a one sentence mention in the local Spanish paper when I won the Infanta Elena riding trophy years ago, to two half-page and a full page in a couple of weeks. Is it surprising I'm divided between a huge grin and total terror?

On top of this, a golfing group calling themselves The Foggies, sponsored us to the tune of 500 euros! Two of the group are directors at the company Mum works for, and they've said they may donate even more if we do well with other sponsors. When we first talked about raising money, Nick and I anticipated total sponsorship of a couple of hundred euros. To get five hundred was a dream, yet now we've received it in a single dollop. Pressure!

I need to focus on studying because if Mum puts a stop to SailAid now it will be seriously embarrassing as well as upsetting. However, I also really want to take my motorbike test on Monday morning which will involve missing a maths test. This is the third time the bike test has been rescheduled and if I don't take it now there's no way I'll manage to do the second part of it before the examining school goes on holiday in August. So, from my point of view, it's vital! My maths teacher won't see it the same way, so I need a note, but to be honest I haven't been doing brilliantly at the subject and may need all my negotiating skills to swing this one. In order to ensure a chilled summer I must pass all eight subjects, but for me, maths is one of the most important as I want to be accepted onto a sea captain's training course in the UK and they specifically look at maths ... but, having used every cent of Christmas and birthday money on my theoretical and practical motorbike course, I don't want to be foiled by the timing of a single test, which I could take any time. It's a serious conundrum.

Another thing that's worrying me is the amount of water Rocky is taking in. Nick says it's normal, but I reckon we have a leak. If Nick's correct, we have a problem. With the additional water the boat will be too heavy to haul up the beach and angle correctly to drain the water out. It's hard enough on a slipway with a trailer, but in sand it will be nearly impossible. Also, with so much water, we won't be able to leave Rocky moored and start sailing again the next morning. She will become increasingly low in the water and there's very little freeboard as it is. This is something we definitely have to sort out properly or it could jeopardise everything. We're going to start by putting more silicone around all the screw heads that go into the hull and anywhere else we can think of. If that doesn't cure it, we'll have to devise a system to find hairline cracks.

Nick: In addition to suspected leaks and regular gales preventing us from getting sufficient training in, we have another concern which we need to tackle. This is our almost total lack of unaided sight.

For several years my closest family and friends have believed the nickname "Cyclops" demonstrates affection. Before the genetic condition of Marfyn's Syndrome was conclusively ruled out as the cause of my eye problems, it had been "Mutant Cyclops", and there was a degree of sadness when the first word had to be dropped. My family pride themselves on being honest, if not kind! Seb, on the other hand, is just blind.

On land we have no problems using glasses and lenses – or "lens" in my case. But at sea, spectacles become rapidly salt encrusted and lenses require fiddly little pots and cleaning fluid every night, neither of which are good on sandy beaches or crashing around in the bottom of small boats. If we want to sail 160 nautical miles and not take a wrong turn, we need some help – cue drum roll "They should have gone to Specsavers!"

We had no doubt about what we needed, it was just how to procure it, and who was going to do the unpleasant task of asking for it, that we were debating. Fate decided to let Seb off the hook when a reminder for my next eye test dropped into the post box, and Mum announced she'd be taking me to Santa Ponca Specsavers the following Thursday.

"You know I would have done it," Seb said down the phone, although I could hear the grin in his voice, "but you might as well ask for a month's supply of daily lenses for both of us while you're there."

The whole idea of asking random people for expensive favours is pretty nerve-wracking, and I spent the preceding week playing "the eye test scene" through in my head to find the optimum time to make my pitch. In my mental cinema this occurred just after "Hola, como estas", when my sympathetic optician helpfully asked what was new in my life since the last visit, allowing me to pop the question before we started on the serious business of reading small letters.

On the way there Mum thought it would be reassuring to tell me that "the worst they can do is say "no"". It wasn't.

I pushed open the door feeling rather hotter than

usual and with a nervousness I generally reserve for the exam room. Within seconds my ever-friendly optician had done the "Hola, como estas" bit, but instead of progressing down the script I had planned for her, she asked how school was going, about my pets, what I had done during the Easter holidays and a host of other very pleasant, but wholly irrelevant, things until we were straight into, "Read the bottom line, please."

There was never a break in the flow of questions and answers. Never an opportunity to veer off the track and onto SailAid. With every passing minute, panic was rising further up my chest as I realised there might never be a chance to recite my prepared speech. Then we were standing up and she was holding the door open for me, efficiently sweeping me out towards the street.

Maybe I moved more slowly than usual towards the door; maybe there was a pleading look in my eyes; maybe I even moaned with frustration, or perhaps it was pure luck that she, finally, threw me a life belt.

"Is there anything else?"

"Well, yes ..." I began, and the speech came tumbling out.

Although it had been so long in coming, it was in fact the perfect time as, with the door open, the other staff in the shop soon heard what I was saying and I was quickly surrounded by Spanish, English and German opticians all asking pertinent questions and not batting an eyelid at my request for free lenses.

The Specsavers' directors seemed to love the idea of "Very Nice People" and our blog, so it was arranged that once our lenses were ready we would come in together to be fitted with them, as they're slightly different to wear than conventional ones, and so they advised us to try them for a week before our trip.

When we went in together, we had photos taken with the directors alongside our multi-lingual "Very Nice Person" signs, and we promised to send copies to them plus a link to the blog.

Unfortunately Mum was having a serious gadget problem with her iPhone camera – she hadn't noticed it was on video! – but was too embarrassed to say anything, so we only got one decent photograph despite a good five minutes of standing with fixed smiles both inside and outside the shop.

Finally Mum managed to take a photo, but not before the smiles had become completely fixed!

However, the blindness issue is solved, and even if the rest of me becomes unacceptably filthy, my eyes (note the "s" please family!) should be crystal clear.

Now we needed to work out how we could beat the constant bad weather and still sail when it was blowing a hooley.

After several attempts at sailing off the slipway with the boom crashing around our heads and the jib flapping like crazy, I was relieved when Dad said he thought we should have a couple of reefing points put in the mainsail.

"There can be some strong flukey winds around the north coast, so I'd feel happier if you started out each day with the reefs in," he explained. "We'll take it to Franco's Dad on Monday and see if he can do it before next weekend."

Franco is a friend of my brother Chris, and his Dad, Miguel, owns the Velas Ferrà sail loft.

Miguel is a massively enthusiastic, ever-smiling Argentinian who greeted my parents with open arms and ardent back slaps. This was despite the fact that when Dad had rung up to arrange the job, Miguel's secretary was having none of it.

"¡Imposible!" she intoned. They were swamped under mountains of super yacht sails, cushion covers and biminis, with several staff already working seven days a week in order to get all the boats up and running in time for the season.

Dad's not known as the "F***ing Aries" for nothing, so he thanked her for her help and promptly rang Miguel's mobile direct.

"¡Ningún problema!" came the reply, the job would be done by Thursday or Friday.

Our worn and grubby piece of canvas promptly skipped to the front of the queue of clients who were all happy to pay thousands of euros for the company's expert attention, and by mid-week two neat lines of reefing points had been punched into place.

When Dad went to pick it up, Miguel was out on a job. After apologising to the secretary for bulldozing our sorry piece of cloth into their state-of-the-art workshop specifically against her wishes, he took out his wallet and asked for the bill.

"No, no Señor," she said with a big smile, "the boss says "no charge", tell the boys "good luck" from all of us."

Dad's guilty feelings at pressurising the Velas Ferrà team in the first place, immediately doubled! What incredibly Nice People! Now we need to get afloat and see how it sets.

Deciding the depth of reefing points we could put into Rocky's mainsail. After Vela Ferrà had put in two rows of eyes, the sail set perfectly.

Seb: I wanted to sort out the leak question before we went sailing again so we knew if we had cured the problem. Pete agreed to help us after work on Friday, so directly we got out of school we put together our "leak buster" kit and hauled it into the boot of the car.

Our contraption consists of Pete's homebrew barrel filled with water plus a couple of bottles of food colouring. We've attached a long hose to the barrel's tap and our idea is to tilt Rocky's bow downwards and syphon red liquid into the hollow part of the hull through the stern bung. Once all the water is inside we'll put the bung back in, gently tip her horizontal again and look for any tell-tale red drips.

Luckily when we arrived at the boatyard the owner of the next door boat wasn't around, so we were able to use his higher stern as a syphoning platform. All went according to plan and we were rewarded with a Eureka moment when red water started bubbling out of the edges around the drainage bung.

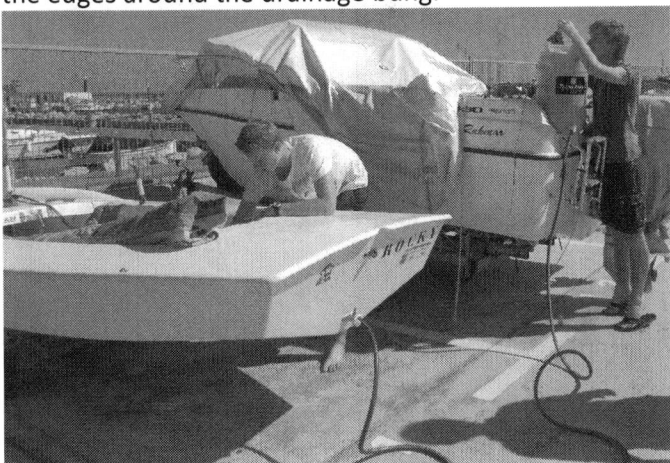

Siphoning coloured water from Pete's beer-making barrel into Rocky to check for leaks.

We drained all the water out and left her to dry overnight.

Early on Saturday morning we were back at the boatyard splurging silicon all around the bung and anywhere else that might have leak potential. We need to ensure she stays dry so she's as easy as possible to right if we capsize.

By the time the wind came up everything was dry and we were ready to try our newly reef-able mainsail. It set perfectly and the smaller sail area gave us the confidence to press Rocky as hard on the wind as she would go. We really put her through her paces, which led to a few white knuckle moments, but we are far happier with how she's handling. Unfortunately neither of us are at our best early in the morning and we managed to forget our hats – it had been cool when we left. We both arrived home looking like English tourists on Day 2 of their holiday.

Chart work after a long day sailing ... we suffered from too much sun that night!

In spite of our sore necks and faces there was no rest as Pete put us through a succession of navigation tests on the old charts we had sliced up into A4 sections last week. After marking them all with latitude and longitude lines, we had them laminated by Kay at the bookshop in Portals, and they are now great mini-charts for a mini-boat.

However, the effects of the sun on our necks was far from over; Nick began violently dry retching before we got to bed, and I was going the whole hog. The next few hours were spent in a haze of trips to the bathroom. Luckily Pete slept right through the unnatural amount of activity going on throughout the night, which was a relief as there was nothing we could do except wait for normality to return, and this wouldn't have been made any better by someone saying "you won't forget your hats again, will you?" which, believe me, was absolutely definitely true!

With Steph and Little Alice away for the weekend, Pete was unrelenting in giving us his full waking attention, so we were back on the water by 11am on Sunday, this time with full sail up and pushing Rocky even harder. After an "unplanned disembarkation" by Nick – he fell out, but managed a polite "Sorry guys!" as he disappeared over the side – Pete immediately decreed that next weekend we will do capsize and man-overboard drills until they are second nature. He's forbidden any further wimping out because the water's still slightly chilly. Next Saturday we all get wet!

As we came back into port we were flying along until there was a loud "twang" that sent a shudder down the mast, as our speed halved and the jib dropped into the water. The halyard had snapped. It couldn't have happened in a better place! With its demise, every major rope will have been replaced by the time we leave, which is quite reassuring!

After a late lunch, where we finally had to admit our stomachs still couldn't face more than a single slice of pizza, it was back to the house. Unfortunately, there was still no pleasant slobbing out on the sofa with some mindless TV watching.

Homework, and other things our mums would view as essential, couldn't get in the way of Pete's drive to achieve as much as possible in 48 female-free hours, so, knackered and salty we sat in the kitchen practicing knots until every bowline was perfect, clove hitches could be done in our sleep and reef knots never ended up as "grannies". Finally it feels as if we'll be ready to go.

Nick: Although Dad wanted capsize and man overboard drill on the following weekend, I was right in the thick of exams and there was no way I could take a whole day off studying – which is what it would have involved. I've always wanted to be a vet and I know how competitive it is to get onto the course at university. SailAid was important to me, but not sufficiently important to override that!

Despite the lack of sailing, we did fit in a few things. Finally we acquired a second paddle. Little Alice had been giving English classes to a boy who lived opposite us for several years. The boy's Dad, Rafa Bujosa, owns the chandlery and second-hand nautical store in Palma called Merca Nautic. As our families knew each other well, it wasn't too daunting to ask if we could put posters up about sponsoring us in his shop windows.

There's an unmistakable misty look of longing that comes into the eyes of some adults when we mention what we're doing. Rafa was one of them.

He dove into his Aladdin's cave of nautical goodies, intent on satisfying all our needs, including those we didn't know we had. Between poster sticking, paddle finding and producing an amazing life-raft knife that could cut through rope, gut fish and generally save your life, yet not puncture anything, Rafa told me that when he was just 14 years old he canoed around Mallorca. This sounded like far more work than sailing! By the time he was 17 he had set sail on a small boat for Barcelona.

Nick with Rafa and the life-raft knife.

As had happened with Captain Kevin, a roguish twinkle blossomed in Rafa's eyes as he recounted his teenage voyages, and I felt completely humbled once again. Before any mobile phones or GPS, these guys, whom I've always thought of as mere friends of my parents, got out there and lived their dreams. There wouldn't have been any PLB signals going off if they got into trouble, they just wouldn't arrive home again. I'm slightly shocked at how doing SailAid has made me realise how many assumptions I make about people around me, and how many of them are far more interesting than I've given them credit for. I've always liked Rafa, but now he's taken on hero-status.

Seb, me and the mums went to see Brad Robertson at his house in the middle of rural Mallorca the following Sunday afternoon, which gave me a couple of hours' study break.

Through our love of diving, we've known Brad for years, but since he set up the marine conservation association, Ondine, our times with him have been even more interesting. He's certainly infected both of us with his passion for protecting the island's underwater health.

"Seeing as you guys have decided to set sail on the day my daughter's due to be born, I may not be around to wave you off," he said with a broad grin. "So I thought you should come round and we could work out how you can help Ondine's projects, and then whatever happens we can get together for a debrief when you arrive back."

Brad asked us to track two things on the waterproof paper and pencils he provided us with.

The first is rubbish. In addition to bagging up as much beach rubbish as we can find when we make camp each night, we'll also be recording what we see in the water. Obviously we'll pick it up if we can, but even just mapping it, together with noting the wind direction and any distinguishing marks, can tell eco-warriors like

Silke Bommersheim, who works closely with Brad, where it's come from and alert them to the danger of it polluting one of Mallorca's five marine reserves.

"We also need you to log megafauna," Brad said, once we had exhausted rubbish.

"Megafauna?"

"Big fish to you mate! Note down the date, time, weather conditions and GPS coordinates of any large animals you see. Although, if it's a Great White, forget all that and just call me immediately!"

I didn't mention it, as I was meant to be in a serious meeting, but if I see any "megafauna" I'm likely to have my mouth and eyes stretched open to their fullest extent, while squeaking "Oh My God!" several octaves higher than usual, rather than doing any of the things I was sagely nodding my head to. I hope I'd grab a camera, but it's more likely I'd only do anything sane after all wondrous beasts had left the scene.

Brainstorming megafauna with Brad and Silke

I really hope our waterproof paper will be full of records of dolphins, rays and turtles. I have no idea how depleted the sea around the island may have become and if we'll see anything at all, but I certainly dream about it. As we left, we promised Brad's wife, Bea, that we wouldn't tell him about any sharks until she assures us all his paternal duties are fulfilled and he's free to jump in a boat and race off to have a look for himself. She was pretty grateful about that!

Best of British

Seb: We've just had a poem written for us and posted on our Facebook page. It's by people in England who are sponsoring us and whom we don't even know! Needless to say, it's brought a massive lump to my throat and, if I didn't have to study every moment of the day, I'd probably get totally freaked out at the level of interest there is, even from so far away.

The poem is by Sue and Alan Wilkinson and it goes:
"May the waters be calm
May the clouds disappear,
Stay safe from all harm,
And suffer no fear.

You have courage in spades,
And kindness within.
We hope for good days.
Bless the boat you are in."

They ended by wishing us "Good luck on your adventure". What amazingly nice people!

At the same time as we received the poem, we discovered Brad had nominated us to win a Best of British award that the local newspaper is running in conjunction with the restaurant chill out spot, Moods, in Portals.

I'm not sure how I feel about this as, although I have a British passport, almost all my time is spent speaking Spanish or Catalan. Also we really want to encourage the Spanish to become enthusiastic about SailAid and not see it as a weird English thing that can be ignored as "foreign". Small scale sponsorship is not understood in Spain. Most charities survive by seeking backing from government agencies or big businesses, so the idea that when lots of people give a little it can add up to what a business would pay out, is completely alien here. I'm worried that if we're seen as too British we may not get the message across that we want to.

"I don't really feel British," I said to Mum.

"You're more siestas and fiestas than Bulldog and Yorkshire puddings!" Mum agreed. "I don't think you should worry about it, after all Dr. Stoma's also been nominated and I'm pretty sure he's Canadian!"

She was right. There were seven other nominees, all of them at least double our age, most much older than that, so the chances of us winning were almost zero, and I already had enough to stress about. It was cool of Brad to have given us his vote of confidence. That gave me the warm fuzzy feeling, even though some of the other nominees were heavy weight philanthropists I felt unworthy to compete against.

Obviously Dr. Stoma had been nominated for his "tireless work for the poor", but there were also nominations for Melinda Lynam who has spent years rescuing animals that have been abandoned and mistreated on the island; there was also a nomination for Tony Insull who is trying to remedy the problems of prostitution and illegal traders in Magalluf. Other nominees were the journalist Andrew Ede; musician Philip Richard Dawson; good Samaritan Bernard Smith; and local councillor Angela Guerrero. People have until next Monday afternoon to vote for their favourites and then the results will be revealed at 3pm on Thursday, 20th of June. This is exactly one hour after my last exam, so it's lucky Moods is just across the road from my school. If it hadn't been so close I would have had no chance of getting there.

With exams every day, Pete's not going to get his capsize drill this weekend either. This is worrying as we're less than a month away from leaving. As Pete's meant to go to sea on the evening of the 22nd June; we're going to have to sail that morning, come hell or high water.

We've had a stroke of luck with the PLB. The company in England got confused and instead of sending one, as Pete and Steph had ordered, they sent two plus an impressive survival first aid kit, strobe lights and many other outward bound bits. Once the PLBs have been registered with the Maritime Coastguard Agency, we will be locatable 100% of the time, even if we become separated. We thought about ringing the company and telling them they'd made a mistake, but we didn't want to confuse them further! (Three months afterwards they realised and Pete and Steph had to pay for the second PLB because it had already been registered. So far, there's been no mention of all the rest of the stuff.) Our safety measures are now as comprehensive as we can make them. Pete's bosses have loaned us two lightweight manual gas lifejackets, and we have bought a tube of cream for jellyfish stings which was the only thing missing from the first aid kit.

Although we don't have time to sail, we are taking Saturday morning off from studying to do our first radio interview and then go to collect some special SailAid t-shirts a local company has had made for us.

By the time Saturday actually arrived, the competition in the Best of British award was getting slightly ugly. Supporters of one candidate had posted that the local councillor shouldn't have been nominated because she was "only doing her job"; supporters of another, claimed Dr. Stoma should be disqualified for being the wrong nationality. Some of the expatriate community were clearly taking this bit of feel-good summer fun a tad too seriously. To our surprise, we were doing OK, lying third behind Melinda, the animal lady, and the local councillor. However, we reckoned many of our votes were from the supporters of Dr. Stoma who were hedging their bets in case the nationality issue really kicked off. The prize for winning was 250 euros for the charity of the winner's choice, so if either we or Dr. Stoma won, the money would go to Mediterranea.

When I walked through Nick's front door 20 minutes before our telephone interview with Talk Radio Europe was due to begin, I was completely calm and enjoying the day. Nick bounded out of the kitchen, "Thank god you're here! They've already been on the phone!"

"I haven't missed it, have I?" I asked, mildly bemused at how jumpy he seemed to be.

"No, they just wanted to check the line. Are you nervous??!"

"No, why?"

"Are you sure you're not nervous??!"

By this time I was beginning to think I should be nervous.

"We mustn't forget to mention Specsavers." It was their PR department that had organised the interview for us. They were pretty switched on that way.

"They're bound to question us about them, aren't they?" I replied over my shoulder while having a quick pre-interview fridge rummage.

"Yes, probably, but in case they don't maybe we should devise some sign language to get the message in. Are you really sure you're not nervous Dude?"

"I wasn't until you kept going on!" I said, as Steph got practical and lined up a couple of phone extensions for us, while Pete tuned in the upstairs radio.

"I'm really nervous."

"I'd have never known!"

I hadn't expected him to react like this, I thought interviews would be right up his street. Nick loves talking so much we'd once had to put duck-tape over his mouth to make him shut up for a minute. This should be his dream!

When the phone rang he leapt for it like a woodland sprite, but after a slightly squeaky start we settled down and did OK by pointing at which of us should speak next. The questions were asked by a studio audience of kids and teenagers. Everything was going smoothly until the final question which was, "Do you have any sailor stories?"

Panic gushed out of Nick's eyes, and I reckoned mine were doing much the same. The horror of a lengthy radio silence punctuated only by the occasional, "Umm, well ..." loomed. I could see white knuckles gripping Nick's receiver when a lance of inspiration struck, "Nick fell out of the boat the other day ..." and I was off, my tightly knotted stomach was untying itself and Nick was grinning and giving me thumbs up signs.

"That was awesome!" Little Alice yelled down the stairs when the presenter cut to a music break. Our first live interview was over and we hadn't sounded like complete idiots. Pete had recorded it and by the time we set off for the Kip McGrath centre in Son Vida to collect our T-shirts, he was already busy uploading it onto our blog.

Kip McGrath offer an array of study techniques

and academic help which, over the years, several of the five of us had used. So, when they heard of our plans, they sponsored us, had stickers made to go on Rocky and had six T-shirts made with SailAid on the front and their logo on the back.

With Julie at Kip McGrath – who is a Very Nice Person.

The T-shirts are great and we spent 20 minutes posing with the centre's owners, Jay and Julie, while Steph and PR guru Vicki McLeod took endless photos. Then we were ushered in to speak to a class of young children who had all been peeking through the windows to find out what was going on.

After introducing us and telling the kids about SailAid, Jay asked if any of her pupils had questions. We fielded the first couple easily enough and then it was the turn of the girl with bunches.

"Where are you going to go to the toilet?" she began as we were swiftly thanked for our time and shown the door. As it was nearing midday there were several parents standing around in reception, some of whom seemed to know about SailAid.

"You could win that competition if you were better at using social media," one of them said as we were leaving.

"Did you hear that old woman?" Nick cried as we got to the privacy of the car park.

"She looked barely over 40," Steph huffed.

"As I said! An old lady telling two teenagers to learn how to use social media!"

"It was pretty cheeky," I admitted.

"But we can't go asking all our friends to vote for us, can we?" Nick said slowly.

"If you put it in terms of "if we win there's an extra 250 euros for Mediterranea" you can," Mum piped up. "You could ask them to vote either for you or Dr Stoma, that wouldn't seem arrogant."

"Maybe," Nick replied as I tried to rationalise an inward squirm that was making my way up from my stomach. We decided to try pushing it a bit and see how things pan out over the rest of the weekend.

Nick: : I went home with my three new T-shirts and took Thumper down the garden. Lying on my back on the grass while he periodically nibbled my toes, I closed my eyes and breathed in deeply. My exams were over, there was nothing more I could do, only time would tell if I had what it takes to do the five A levels I want. Now, for the first time in many months, I had nothing to do until Monday morning, when I was to start a week of work experience at Calvia Vets.

For a while I couldn't relax. Although my brain

was telling me all the action was over, buried in my chest there was a panicky feeling that I'd forgotten something vital; that I was on the point of waking up and remembering that my most important exam was in half an hour and I'd done no revision. I tried to breathe deeper and slower. My heart needed to stop thundering away beneath my ribs and chill a bit. Thumper hopped up my arm and settled down to be stroked; eventually we drifted into a doze together.

By the time I ambled back to the house and had a look at Facebook, Seb had already been busy brushing up his social media skills. That made me feel a bit of a slacker, so I got to work asking people to share our nomination page and vote for us. When I looked an hour later our efforts had been worth it, we were nearly level pegging with the local councilor, so I fired off a few more messages and nudged the Alices to get their friends involved too.

Suddenly the local councilor surged thirty "likes" ahead. There was no doubt she had noticed our social media efforts! None of the other contestants were moving much. Melinda, the animal rescuer, was very popular but had only picked up a handful of fresh "likes" today as voting had now been underway for a while. I texted Seb, "Do you think we're being given social media lessons by another old woman?"

"Could be!" he replied "Should we try a bit harder?"

In the next couple of hours we got serious. Every time we began to close the gap, within half an hour she had procured an extra twenty or thirty "likes". After the fourth time, I was getting frustrated.

"Bloody hell she's good at this," I said to Mum as our opponent ploughed through the 200 "likes" barrier.

"Don't beat yourself up about it," Mum replied. "She's a politician, if she couldn't persuade loads of people to vote for her she wouldn't have a job."

"But we're young! We're meant to be computer kings!"

She just grinned at me and raised an eyebrow. Mum doesn't do competitiveness which at times like this can be pretty annoying.

Political corruption is constantly in the news here at the moment, so the notion that we were being beaten by a politician began to get up a number of influential noses and we inched steadily forward. By the time I went to bed I reckoned I had begged every "like" and "share" I was likely to get.

Sunday morning dawned and we'd been thoroughly overtaken once again. There was now just us and Angela Guerrero, the local councilor, in the running. Melinda was in third place and Dr. Stoma was a long way behind.

"Looks like I'm going to be spending all day chasing the politician," I said at breakfast. Mum gave me the eyebrow treatment again.

"It's a beautiful day. You've just finished your exams, and you want to spend the day indoors staring at a screen?"

"No, but Seb's studying so I ought to ..."

"Rubbish! Go to the beach. Dr. Stoma wouldn't want you to vegetate for an entire Sunday on the off chance that you just might win; get it in perspective."

I felt a bit torn, it wasn't that I wanted to stick around the house, but Ms. Guerrero was playing an exceedingly irritating game and I was loath to admit defeat. Mum might not understand a competitive nature, but the rest of us sure as hell do! However, the sun was shining, the sky was blue, the sea was warm, and I had no more studying to do. I grabbed a towel and ran for the bus.

When I returned a small miracle had occurred. Some Facebookers with seriously large numbers of online friends were beating their drums for us. While I swam and played volleyball, somehow we had eased into the lead.

By Monday morning we were fifteen "likes" behind again.

"Never mind, it's over," I mumbled through a mouthful of Weetabix, while trying to sound stoical. "I'm at work until seven and Seb has exams all day so there's nothing more we can do about it."

"What's that?" Chris asked. He'd been out most of the weekend and had completely missed the Battle of the Likes.

"We're being beaten by a politician in the Best of British award and voting ends at five this afternoon."

"Beaten by a politician?" He was beginning to wake up, "on Facebook?"

"Yes, but it's no big deal, she's a pro."

"I haven't asked any of my friends …" I could actually see the effect of caffeine coursing its way through his body as he took his second gulp of coffee, this was a good sign.

"Well, if you're not too busy, that would be great …"

"I'm not working until one, consider it done bro!"

At ten past five my phone started vibrating constantly in my pocket. The moment we were between animals I sneaked a look. Voting had ended and we were ahead by almost 40 "likes". An hour later we realised we'd been outclassed once again. We'd been so focused on the Facebook count that we'd forgotten people could also vote by email and snail-mail. The organisers posted a message that there were a large number of these and the final count would be announced at the award ceremony on Thursday.

"I don't reckon we'll have a single email vote," I said to Seb. "We missed a trick there."

"Never mind, the whole thing gave SailAid more publicity than we could have ever hoped for. It was definitely worth it."

Seb can be rather wise at times, although I never admit it to his face.

"At least we'll see Brad and Dr. Stoma at the awards, and if all the nominees turn up we should meet the animal lady."

"Yes, she seemed cool. See you Thursday."

By the next morning things had changed. Brad had become a Dad. The pictures he sent through of Bea and baby Naia were painfully beautiful. Ever since Bea became pregnant, Brad's drive to preserve the underwater world for future generations went up several notches, now you could almost hear him crash into overdrive. Mum, Diane and the Alices were already in full flow volunteering themselves for babysitting duties, but Brad seemed so smitten we thought that even a whole shoal of Great Whites wouldn't entice him away from his family. Consequently we were gob-smacked when he turned up at Moods on Thursday. We definitely did not expect him to keep that promise.

My lunch break was from 1.30 to 3pm, so I had asked Juan and Anna at Calvia Vets if I could take an extra half hour and they were great about it. By 2.30 Seb and I were in Moods car park hastily changing into our new SailAid T-shirts. Inside, all our families were there with the exception of Big Alice who couldn't get time off work. Captain Kevin had arrived with Dad and Chris. His gravelly voice was informing people that he was willing to use his walking stick on any politician who trounced his "young men". Dr. Stoma was smiling benignly and Brad was being congratulated by everybody while sporting a grin so wide it must have made his cheeks ache.

With British punctuality, Margaret Whittaker, the owner of Moods, and Jason Moore, the editor of the Majorca Daily Bulletin, began their speech. We were in a huddle with all the other nominees, apart from the local councilor who had chosen to stand on the opposite side of the area. The speakers detailed a close run competition and as we were about to bring our hands together for Angela Guerrero, the editor turned to look at Captain Kevin and with a friendly smile announced, "The winners are the SailAid boys, Sebastian Page Franklin and Nick Mason."

Nick, Dr. Michael Stoma, Seb, New-Dad Brad, Pete and Chris Mason with the Best of British award.

Our families aren't known for being reserved, so there was an explosion of cheering and a fair few of Alice's piercing whoops. But as we moved forward to collect our trophy a man, in a cream shirt with black swirls on it, turned to face us and said in a thunderous voice, "This is outrageous! Ridiculous! They haven't even done anything yet!"

I kept smiling but my eyes met Alice's and I could see she had heard and wasn't happy. Mum touched my arm, "Don't worry babe, you've done great." But I couldn't help feeling that this man was right and that Melinda, Tony Insull and Dr. Stoma had done so much over so many years that most people would see our win as a travesty.

"Not true," Dr Stoma said as we were herded across to where the photos were being done. "You've had to do a lot for this already, and people were voting for young people with consciences. They were voting for the future."

Melinda was awesome. We both felt she should have won it for her personality alone. She never stopped congratulating us. All the other nominees were being really kind too and then Margaret Whittaker announced that in addition to the 250 euros she was giving for our charity, she was giving the same again to us.

"That's 125 euros each!" Seb hissed.

"That's more than all my birthdays and Christmases put together!" I whispered back.

"Mine too!"

"I only need 40 to pay off the rest of my debt to Dad for losing his iPhone earphones! I don't know what I'll do with the rest."

"Nor do I. Shall we just take 100 each and give

the extra 50 to Mediterranea? After all our votes were really votes for Dr Stoma."

"Good idea."

Seb was wearing his wise hat again.

Alice was still mad about the man in the cream shirt, "If I'd behaved like that everyone would have said I was hormonal!" she growled, but I couldn't wait around to see if she was going to give him one of her legendary put-downs as I was already late for work. With a final "Thank you" to Margaret Whittaker and a promise to put the logos of her businesses on Rocky, I was running out of the door with Mum, ready to make my apologies to Juan and Anna.

Seb: Nick dashed passed me with a "see you later, mate!" We are going up to Pollensa directly he leaves work to see some people who are offering to help us when we get to the North of the island. As he disappeared out of the door, a wave of urgency came over me to get out of the crowd and find some space to think in.

I took out my mobile and called the student I was meant to give an English lesson to. I never usually cancel classes, but having finished all my exams and won Best of British in the space of an hour, I was going to make an exception.

Mum was saying her goodbyes to Brad and Captain Kevin. "Can you give me a lift into the village?" I asked.

"If you come right now, I've got to get back to work."

That suited me.

As I walked through the centre of Portals village, I

felt completely shell-shocked. Summer was finally here. I'd passed my motorbike test and the other exams seemed to have gone OK. I had money in my pocket and on Sunday I was booked onto the ferry to Menorca where I would fulfill one of my greatest dreams – to go to the Sant Joan fiestas in Ciudadella.

The celebrations for San Juan on Mallorca are good. Most people head for the beach where they sit within circles of flickering candles, having leisurely picnics until midnight. Then everyone rushes into the sea to swim before the young people stay to sleep on the beach and watch the stars overhead, and the parents head home to comfy beds.

The Mallorcan version is very tame compared to the Menorcan town of Ciudadella where they party for several days and nights. The most spectacular part of these fiestas is the massive black stallions that ornately dressed men ride at dangerous speeds through the narrow cobbled streets. There are jousting competitions on them, and these incredible beasts have been taught to dance on their hind legs through the crowds that are pressing in around them. Until now I have only seen the newspaper pictures every year, in a couple of days I'll actually be there.

It felt as if I was sleep-walking as I started down the small flight of steps into Dr. Stoma's surgery. I was relieved to see a row of empty chairs through the window. I pushed open the door and buckled into a hard wooden seat. Leaning back I stared at the pictures of smiling African faces from the orphanages Mediterranea had set up, the room was cool and silent. I needed this peace. Even when things are going great, like now, I often have to be quiet and take time to sort everything out in my head.

The surgery door opened and the doctor's floppy grey hair appeared in the frame.

"Hello! I didn't expect to see you again today," he said, sinking onto a chair opposite me. "Are you OK?"

"Yes, fine," I replied, relaxing my legs out in front of me. "Pleased to be out of the mayhem though! I've come because we were given a prize for ourselves as well as the charity envelope we gave to you, and we have agreed it is far too much for just us, so we'd like to donate another 50 euros to Mediterranea."

"My goodness, that's incredibly generous of you! Are you sure? You're about to have a three month summer holiday in which to spend it," his eyes were smiling at me so I could easily have changed my mind if I had wanted to.

"I'll be working all of August," I said, getting the note out of my back pocket. "It's great to have extra money for my trip to Menorca, but honestly neither of us needs this much."

Dr. Stoma told me exactly how many cartons of milk our contribution would buy for local children, and it was soothing to hear him talk on about all the charity's projects, with no demands on me other than the occasional nod. When a patient arrived, I took my leave of the air-conditioned tranquillity and re-entered a blistering heat at the bus stop. I had plenty of time to get to the Masons' house before Steph left to pick up Nick and take us both to the northern-most tip of the island.

MOJOs Marine Help, is run by Maureen (Mo) and Joe Fiteni together with Sebastian Danthez. They met us in the modern terraced bar of Pollensa Yacht Club. As well as offering all necessary services for yachts around the Alcudia and Pollensa area, they also run a highly successful Facebook page called Boating in Mallorca which has more than 700 followers.

"You want to try and get round to Cala San Vicente rather than stop in Pollensa," Joe said as we talked about our planned route. "It will cut off a good couple of hours' sailing on your longest stretch down to Cala Sa Calobra. We can still get to you easily by road to bring you food." This last part of the sentence made us very happy indeed.

With the MOJO Marine Help team of Sebastian, Maureen and Joe (L-R) who offered us help at the northern tip of the island.

We had been put in touch with Boating in Mallorca through Brad because they are organising a Second Hand Nautical Fair in mid-October and were determined it shouldn't be solely comprised of endless people trying to sell stuff. Joe had contacted Brad about a film made on the last Great White Shark to be caught off the coast of Pollensa in the 1970s. He had already located the boat involved and arranged for it to be moored at the show, but he needed someone to present the story and, as everyone knows, there's nobody more shark-mad than Brad!

Joe has also arranged for Giacomo de Stefano, aka Forrest Gump in a boat, to be on hand with his films and endless tales about his adventures in the wooden dinghy which he sailed and rowed from London to Istanbul (see www.manontheriver.com)

"Do you think you could get Rocky back up here for the twelfth of October?" Joe asked us, "I'm sure you'll have plenty to tell people about."

This was a bit daunting when we hadn't even done the trip yet. What if it went horribly wrong, or we had nothing much to say? But they had promised food and water, so Nick was already agreeing heartily and pledging to put a power-point presentation together in time for the Boat Show.

Joe, Mo and Sebastian all seem really friendly and the Mums are openly relieved we have nautical folk looking out for us around the trickiest part of the coastline. We drove back via the scenic route as the sun was setting on Alcudia Bay.

It's amazing to think that in a couple of weeks we'll be sailing Rocky up here. The seascape is so beautiful, and yet very different from the south where we come from, even though it is a mere hour's drive away.

Back at the Masons, and by now, completely starving, we were in the kitchen looking at Facebook while Steph cooked dinner.

"Oh my god, she's posted on our SailAid site!" Nick exclaimed.

"Who has?"

"Angela Guerrero! It's all about how Melinda should have won ..."

"Has Melinda said anything?" Steph asked.

"No, she was really nice to us. I don't think she would have anything to do with this, it's just the politician saying she should have given all her votes to her."

"Weird! Just post something about MOJOs and some photos and it will soon work its way down the news column," Steph suggested, but, as she said it, I looked at the screen and up popped the same message, sent a second time.

Within minutes it had arrived for a third time.

"What's she playing at? It's over!" I said.

"It's really negative, we don't want this on our site," Nick said, as Steph came over and poked her head between ours to have a look.

"No, it's not great, is it? Looks as if she's totally lost the plot! Can you wipe them off?"

"Probably, but we can't spend the next few weeks watching what she writes on our site the whole time so we can quickly wipe it."

We really didn't need this aggravation after the long day we'd had. Our blood sugar was at rock bottom and Nick had to be back at work experience first thing in the morning.

"We can ban her from the page," I said as a message landed in front of us.

"It's from her!" Nick began reading, "'Hi Guys I think you must be very proud, dot, dot, dot, your FB campaign was brilliant well done and congratulations

Angie Guerrero' should we reply?" he asked.

"It's not exactly complimentary, but perhaps we should ignore that and just say 'Thank you'", I suggested.

"You think so?"

"... plus a smiley face!" I said with a laugh, "everyone loves a smiley face, and she deserves it!"

"OK go for it," Steph said while draining the pasta, "but then for god's sake ban her from the site before she does herself any more damage! She'll wake up tomorrow and want to bury herself for showing everyone she can't lose to a couple of kids!"

"Done!" said Nick. "Let's eat!"

Final Countdown

Nick: By Friday morning we thought the bizarre Best of British behaviour was over. Wrong.

Every Saturday Angela Guerrero has a weekly column in the Majorca Daily Bulletin, the same daily newspaper that had run the competition with Moods. Bearing in mind that there had been a Friday edition out since our win was announced, the whole thing was already old news, yet the first paragraph of Ms. Guerrero's column was dedicated to it.

"As I have already told you," she wrote, "I was truly delighted to be nominated and that for me, the nomination was every bit as good as winning …"

"Hang on a minute," Seb said when I read it out, "is she saying she won?"

"She's certainly making it ambiguous, look, further down she says 'whatever the outcome ..', has the paper gone weekly and we haven't noticed?!"

"I love this bit!" Seb was almost choking on his cereal as he read out her description of herself when she realised we were seriously practicing our social media skills.

"I myself turned from the cute little smiling Cheshire cat into Shere Khan the tiger …"

"No shit, Sherlock!" I remarked as we grabbed out hats, ready, finally, for a day of capsizing and man overboard drills.

Dad had already decided how today was going to run. He was captain and we were to do as we were told. To begin with, there was no messing around on the slipway with sails.

"Get your hand off that rope and grab a paddle each," he ordered. "Now, one, two, one, two, one, two

..." he commanded while expertly slotting the rudder onto its spindles and bringing us alongside a buoy.

"Sebastian, put a bowline through that ring. Nick, get the mainsail up with the first reef in."

With a few mooted "aye, aye, Captains", we set to work, refusing to quite admit to ourselves that Dad's way might be cooler than the methods we'd been attempting to perfect for weeks. Once the sails were up and the ropes all checked, we slipped the painter from the buoy's ring and headed out.

There was plenty of wind. Even with three of us in her, Rocky was ploughing great furrows in the water while Dad was pressing her harder and harder on the wind.

"She goes like a train," he shouted, a huge grin spreading across his face. "We'll take her into the port basin to capsize her."

"No!" we both replied, "there's too many people there, we should capsize out here."

"The inlet basin is better. The water's deeper and

you'll be protected from being blown further inshore," he argued.

"No, we're not doing that."

It had taken less than 20 minutes for us to become mutineers.

"Have it your way," Dad said handing the helm back to us. "Go ahead and flip her over."

The waves were surging past us as we dug her starboard side hard into the water and sailed her under. There was a confusion of sodden canvas and then I surfaced to see Dad and Seb swimming for their hats before they up-ended them over their heads.

Dad, still in his sunglasses, was pushing us up to stand on the centreplate but we could feel the mast juddering beneath. None of us were in any doubt what was happening, the masthead was bouncing along the bottom and every time it dug itself into the stony sea floor my teeth jangled in my head. We needed to get her upright fast, but without inflicting more damage than we feared we'd already done.

For what seemed like ages she would not respond, and the pounding continued to rise up the mast and through the hull we were trying to balance on. Very slowly we pulled her into a more horizontal position and the water began to slip out of the sails, while the swell washed first me and then Seb, back into the water, time and time again.

"Get back up there," Dad yelled as he trod water beside us, "you don't want the mast going down again."

With ponderous agony she began to right. "Easy! Don't let her flip the other way, she's unstable now."

We dropped into the water as Rocky sat on her bottom once again and wallowed. A giant tangle of sheets tied the jib around the forestay. We threw paddles and bailers back inside the cockpit, then, one by one, we flopped over the side and started to sort her out.

"Not brilliant," Dad commented. "We'll do man-overboard before we try a second capsize in case you do more damage next time."

I rolled my eyes and kept untangling ropes.

Within a few minutes we were surfing the waves again.

"Nick, overboard please!" and I was out and swimming before I'd taken half a breath. Seb carried straight on and I was just beginning to wonder if I'd been talking too much and they'd decided to leave me for an extended period, when Rocky literally drew up alongside and I was back wiggling my toes under the foot straps.

"Seb, out you go," Dad said, as Seb immediately obliged with a splash.

"Keep your eye on him and keep going forward until, when you turn towards him, you'll be on a beat when you aim just slightly upwind of his position. Get him amidships and then allow the boat to drift down onto him and pull him over the lee side."

It worked a treat and Seb was soon back on board.

"The aim is to pick up your crew mate before he's had time to finish peeing," Dad said by way of explanation as we took alternate turns at swimming for what seemed like hours. "Once you can do that you know you're slick at it."

"I reckon it's your turn now, Pete," Sebastian said with a wink at me.

"No, anyone over 50 is exempt," Dad replied.

"Good try Dad ... but no," I said as Seb whipped the sunglasses off the end of Dad's nose while I gave him a hefty shove.

"OK, you know how to do it," Dad conceded as we hauled him back into the boat.

"That's just you being nice because you don't want to go in again," Seb said.

"I'm going to *have* to go in again because you need to do another capsize," Dad countered with a grimace. "This time though, we'll do it where I say, which is inside the port basin."

Neither of us felt capable of arguing any more. We knew we were on a steep learning curve.

Our second capsize was considerably better. The water was deeper so there was no mast po-go-ing, and we'd got the hang of how to coax her horizontal before nursing her upright.

"OK, let's get her back on land and see what damage we've done." This was an instruction neither of us was sorry to have to obey. We drained a ton of water out behind us as we hauled Rocky up the slipway.

"We need to get the mast down," Dad ordered once we'd removed the sails and left them draped over the ground to dry.

The top of the mast looked rather unhappy. There was an evil dent in the side and the sail track was full of sand. It took us 40 minutes to wash all the sand out and then Seb went and borrowed a screwdriver off a nearby boat with which to bend the metal back into shape.

Washing out the mast track before straightening out the dents.

We re-stepped the mast and opened the stern locker to put the baler away before covering her. The locker was empty.

"We've lost the anchor," I announced. There was no sign of any anchor, chain or rope.

"It must have slipped up to the bow in all the

action," Seb reasoned. "Maybe if we tip her gently stern-down, it will slide back again."

With a great deal of heaving we tried that. It didn't work. Then we each tried to squeeze as far as possible into the locker entry hole and stretch our arms to their fullest extent up either side of the hull. Dad could feel absolutely nothing but the tips of Seb's fingers just grazed part of the rope. I could see the edge of the locker sawing into Seb's shoulder as he pressed his arm millimetre by millimetre further down the hull. Sweat was pouring off him and his teeth were gritted in pure concentration. After several minutes of painful wriggling he opened his eyes.

"I've got it," he gasped. Hesitantly he pulled his arm out to reveal a red welt round his shoulder and, eventually, a section of rope in his hand.

We drew the anchor back out and decided that while Seb was in Menorca we would fit a bolt and ring through the stern so that we could put the anchor, and any other sturdy belongings, into shopping bags and tie them to the ring, so they are unable to escape in extreme conditions.

Directly Seb returns we will go on a shake-down voyage to see how far we can get in a full day, then we will camp overnight before returning the following morning. After the way Rocky handled today, I really can't wait.

Seb: Menorca was amazing. Endless crowds of happy people; towering powerful stallions; an atmosphere pulsating with expectation dusted with fear as the horses charged down corridors of people while the rider attempted to spear a tiny ring. If you've never been, look up Sant Joan, Cuidadella, on line and see what you're missing.

We now only have a couple of days before we are due to leave. We must do a trial run, so we packed food, water, tent and sleeping bags and got down to Rocky early in the morning ready to leave on the first zephyr of wind.

We had a point to prove. Pete and Steph keep looking sceptical when we say we're going to reach Cala Pi on the first day. In addition to complicit smiles between the two of them, which are thoroughly annoying, there's even been the words "lucky to get to Arenal" and other negative sentences thrown our way. So, it's Cala Pi or bust.

The other, very secondary (honestly), reason for needing to know if Cala Pi is a possible destination, is that I just *might* have put out a general message that we would be there on the first night. And, I just *might* have invited everyone to join us. My friends have told their friends, who just *might* have told a few additional people, so it really is quite important that we haven't made a massive miscalculation.

We pushed Rocky out towards the slipway. There were already two other boats being launched from trailers attached to 4 x 4s. As we arrived a Guardia Civil van drew up and the officers began demanding to see paperwork from everybody. We stood quietly to one side praying they wouldn't notice us.

"Papeles?" one of the green uniforms said as he approached us. We were both just dressed in swimming trunks, no T-shirts, no shoes, definitely no "papeles".

Luckily after a minimal amount of arm-waving we were able to convince him that, unlike the 4x4 owners, as we were towing Rocky by hand on a flimsy trolley that would never manage a road, it had to be true that we had a spot in the boatyard, and therefore the right to use the slipway.

As a fresh 4x4 arrived, the Guardia lost interest in our lack of available paperwork and we scuttled to the water's edge as quickly as possible.

Once we got out of the port the wind was obliging in its strength, if not in its direction. We had Rocky on a hard beat the whole way, but we kept full sail up and by 4 o'clock we were delighted to see the entrance to Cala Pi appear on the horizon.

We'd been careful to check-off each indent in the coastline on our chart, but all the same we were pretty relieved when we confirmed to each other that we were definitely in the right place. However, as we entered the inlet we realised that this wasn't the best time to arrive. The beach was heaving with families and dense clusters of children were swimming around the yellow-buoyed boat entrance channel.

"I don't think we should go through there," I said to Nick.

"Too right Dude. Let's get the sails down and paddle over that side where there aren't so many people."

It seemed a reasonable idea to us, but as we were about to jump into a clear patch of water and drag Rocky up onto the only free slice of beach, the resident lifeguard starting going completely ballistic. Swinging down from his wooden raised platform like an excitable orang-utan in a red T-shirt, he strode across the sand yelling all the way that we were mentally deficient for going anywhere except the designated boat entrance, and that if we didn't move immediately, to where all the families were, he would call the feared Guardia Civil.

To give him his due, he only allowed his face to show total shock for a fraction of a second when we answered him in perfect Spanish. To be fair, neither of us looks remotely local, so it was no wonder that he thought it would be fine to scream all sorts of insults at us.

We weren't about to argue with him as we were already feeling the effects of the sun in spite of having slapped on gallons of sun block and worn hats constantly. Rocky offers almost no shade and I was worried I was going to suffer a further night of heaving my guts up if I didn't get horizontal beneath a tree and pour a large quantity of water down my throat.

After moving Rocky to where the lifeguard pointed, and inconveniencing about six families in the process, we spent an hour eating the sandwiches we had packed while drinking more than we'd ever done before in one sitting. Unfortunately the lifeguard wasn't finished with us and after a brief pause, in which he rethought his strategy, he returned to inform us that he would, once again, call the Guardia Civil if we stayed for more than six hours. His zealous attention was worrying, and we hoped this wasn't a pattern that would plague us all the way around the island.

"I reckon we should leave," Nick said. Every bone in my body groaned in opposition to this suggestion. "Just until the sun goes down. I bet he's not paid to stay past 7 o'clock and once he goes up all those steps he's not likely to come all the way down again just to see if we've come back."

Nick had a point. It was better to leave now and hope to avoid future hassle. We dragged Rocky back into the water and paddled her around the mass of swimmers and out towards the entrance.

"I can't be bothered to get the sails up again," I said as we hid behind a headland.

"Me neither. Let's just drift and pick up all this floating rubbish. We'll soon see when he's left with a red T-shirt like that."

For two hours we floated and filled most of Rocky's cockpit with the cans and plastic that was washing up against the cliffs. Finally we saw a scarlet-clad form climbing the steps. We left it another 15 minutes before gingerly paddling in to an almost deserted beach.

There were a couple of guys around who looked harmless, so we asked them to give us a hand pulling Rocky further up the beach. By the time we'd emptied her of sand and water we were surrounded by splendid isolation. In the time we'd been bobbing about the entire area had been carpeted by cool shade. The jam of bodies and happy screams had been replaced by total peace, and dusk had begun to creep into the bay. I decided to go exploring while Nick stayed with Rocky. First I investigated the dry river bed, or "torrente" as it's called here, that backed the beach. Next I climbed to the top of the cliffs and looked down to see Nick dozing in the lifeguard's tower. I decided it was time he woke up and took his guarding of Rocky more seriously!

His headless chicken impression when I shouted to him from the cliff top had to be seen to be properly appreciated. Completely disorientated, he ran round in circles several times before he was able to locate where the voice was coming from, so I felt duty bound to take a photo of him when he finally looked in the right direction. It shows just Nick, Rocky and a wide expanse of empty sand. This was what we had been imagining.

Finally Nick worked out where the noise was coming from and stopped running round in circles!

We pitched the tent and lay out our sleeping bags, aware that neither of us was going to manage to stay awake for long.

Then we made a grim discovery. The watermelon

had exploded. It hadn't enjoyed our violent tacking and had disintegrated completely into a mushy sticky gunk that now covered the entire contents of the food bag. The smell was indescribable. Fermenting watermelon is something I could have nightmares about. However many times we washed out the bag in the sea, the smell was still there. All the tins that had sported paper labels were now unnamed, so it was pot luck what we opened for supper. By that point we no longer cared.

As darkness fell it was a race to get into our tent and away from the mosquitos.

It was a very long night. Neither of us slept. If only we could have managed a couple of hours of unconsciousness we would have been slightly recharged, but we had pitched the tent beneath the cliff believing it was the best hiding place from any passing Guardia Civil. However, it was the hardest piece of ground imaginable. We learnt two important things.

Firstly, Carrefour's two-person tent is for vertically challenged people only. We experimented with leaving the door flap open and sticking our feet out, but we were immediately devoured by swarms of hungry insects. So we had to curl ourselves outwards making the sides bulge into an "O" shape. The second revelation was that we are not well-padded. No matter where we wriggled we could not get comfortable and the dark hours were spent in fractured moments of shutting our eyes and praying for sleep, punctuated by searing pain on whatever joints we'd been resting on. We definitely need to find a solution before Saturday.

When the sun drained across the sand at 6 am it was a relief to crawl out of our shelter and stretch. We breakfasted on a few bruised apples and our last tin of beans before picking up the rubbish that people had left on the beach the day before and putting it in the bin.

At 9am we paddled out and hoisted sail. This was well before any lifeguards or sunbathers arrived.

I was completely shattered. I never imagined I would get so tired. I was now seriously worried about the number of people I had told to come to Cala Pi on Saturday night. Not only was there the possible problem of the lifeguard and that all of us might end up being arrested on our first night out, but the whole idea of a party, and then continuing to sail the next day, now seemed really stupid if not actually dangerous.

Completely knackered ... but still sailing.

Thankfully there was little wind for the first hour and I was able to slowly peel my eyes open and become semi-conscious by the time we were hit by a strong breeze. Rocky literally surfed back to Portixol, Nick was on the helm and kept her goose-winging so that we reached seven knots easily much of the time. When we staggered through Nick's front door it was barely lunch time. The incredulous expression on Steph's face when we told her we'd been to Cala Pi and back was truly gratifying, and we would have enjoyed it for longer if we had been able to remain upright and awake.

Now I need to try to dissuade a large number of people, some of whom I don't know, from taking any notice of my open invitation to join us for a night on the beach!

Nick: With only one day before we leave, everything has gone into overdrive. Brad has finally obtained the Ondine sign to go on our mainsail and Mum is panicking that the sail won't fit under her sewing machine, so we're on stand-by to hand stitch it, which will take us well into the night.

We've just received sixteen more stickers to put on the hull, some of them over a metre long. Teo, of Palma Media, who made all the stickers, gave us a tip. He told us that we need to cover both Rocky and the back of the sticker in plenty of soapy water so we can move them around and get them straight before leaving them to dry and harden. Hopefully this will stop us from creating any more artistic horrors like Seb's diagonal stern sticker.

We've been out and bought food, water and li-los, which we hope will help with our sleeping problem. Since the shake down trip we've discovered that we can't get half the things we thought we needed into our two dry bags. Sleeping bags, sun block and the first aid kit are essential, but more than one spare T-shirt, fishing tackle and a torch are not. We have a hand-held compass and the PLBs, a little money and Seb's smartphone – carefully wrapped in layer after layer of guaranteed waterproof bags.

A long distance sailor called Florian Gander has lent us a small solar panel which will charge our phones. He found our blog and by chance was about to pass through Palma, so he offered to drop off this marvelous gadget. We had anticipated we would need to spend a lot of time and leg work finding friendly bars that would allow us to plug in for a few hours. This would mean one of us would have to stay at the bar while the other stayed with Rocky. However, if the solar panel works half as well as Florian assures us it does, our problems are solved. His boat is due to return to Palma in August and he's kindly said we can keep it until then. Fantastic!

Although everything seems manic at the moment, I know we'll be on the slipway by 9am tomorrow because we have to be in time to meet a journalist from the local Spanish newspaper, Ultima Hora. Somehow we'll make it!

Day One

Seb: Mum drove me to Portixol early in the morning. We arrived just in time to see Nick launch Pete out of the boat and into the sea.

"What did you do that for?"

"He's the worst paddler in history! He kept going round and round in circles while telling me what to do! If you'd arrived on time, I wouldn't be half-knackered before we've even started."

The parents went off in search of breakfast. Nick clearly hadn't had a great start to his day. Once again the Guardia Civil had shown up asking for paperwork, but this time Nick could recite his exact berth number and had Pete to back him up.

A few people had said they were coming down to see us off and a journalist from the largest Spanish newspaper on the island, Ultima Hora, was due to arrive at 10.

Rocky looked great in her new stickers and with long Mediterranea and Ondine flags streaming from the crosstrees. It was a perfect morning; completely calm, sunlight glinting off the sea with a cloudless turquoise sky.

The first thing we did after pulling Rocky up the small-stone beach was to attach Pete's QR codes to the mast for the English and Spanish blog sites. It was the last thing he'd done before he left for sea, and as he'd taken a couple of hours away from work and come and see us off, we thought we should put them on prominent display. It was sheer chance that Capella, the boat Pete is captain of, was still on the island and we were really glad he was there to see us leave – whether or not he was useless at paddling.

We took some time packing and re-packing Rocky so that eventually we had a small pile of things we reckoned we could do without. If we were wrong, we hoped to be able to ask someone to bring them to wherever the boat was, but as it turned out we found we needed fewer and fewer things as time went by.

Packing and re-packing ready to leave, the Best of British award is perched on the bow.

Gabriel Alomar from Ultima Hora arrived on time and began taking photographs and asking us questions. After answering the obvious ones about what we were doing, and why, both Nick and I dried up. I could only focus on Rocky, and by that stage I just wanted to leave, to get out to sea, to start what we'd been planning for months. Being made to wait for a further 30 minutes to tick by felt like an eternity.

Mum materialised by the side of Señor Alomar

and began telling him all the things she knew he needed to know, while looking over his shoulder to check he was spelling names correctly. She's really good at that sort of thing and within minutes it was obvious she had him under her spell and he was scribbling so fast the pages of his notebook were flying over every few seconds.

Steph was dishing out watermelon to the small crowd that had gathered on the beach, but both Nick and I couldn't stomach anything and continued to tinker with the boat as the minute hands on our watches crawled painfully slowly towards 11 o'clock.

Pete was giving us last minute tips, as was Captain Kevin O'Regan. By 10.55 we'd had enough, and so we began the goodbye hugging. We were swiftly pushed out to sea, sails ready hoisted. We did two short tacks out, and on the second one, the five screws holding the starboard jib track in place pulled right out of the hull and crashed onto the cockpit floor. All our friends and family were still waving and whistling less than 50 metres away.

"Holy crap!" Nick exclaimed while trying to keep the jib in a vaguely normal place for the benefit of the on-loookers who were still busy with their cameras.

Meeting each other's eyes we chorused in complete unison, "We're not going back!"

Once that was decided, we used the foot-strap as a makeshift track. It wasn't brilliant but it was better than nothing, and monumentally better than telling anyone what had occurred while we were still at the point where the sensible response would be, "Come back to shore ..."

After an hour we phoned in and admitted what had happened, and that we'd left both the GPS and the camera in the car. The good thing was that as Steph would now have to bring tools and West System to Cala Pi, it was one hundred per cent certain she'd bring food too and so we wouldn't need to eat tins tonight. The down side was the feeling that we hadn't yet quite escaped.

We enjoyed a good sail and luckily were using the port jib track most of the way. When we reached the entrance to Cala Pi we didn't even bother going in. For nearly two hours we jibed and tacked in the waters outside until we were quite certain the lifeguard had gone.

It had already been a long day in the sun, but we were becoming better at keeping hydrated and as we finally heard the crunch of sand beneath Rocky as she glided onto the beach, we didn't feel anywhere near as exhausted as we had the previous time.

Nick: When Mum arrived with tools and West System there were a handful of friends already on the beach and we were feeling pretty relaxed. Little Alice decided she should be the handy-woman, which we were fine about until Mum's growing frustration became clear, and she sent Alice and her friend Jade off to pitch the tent and blow up li-los.

"Right! I don't want to be here all night, so leave your friends for a minute and focus on this …"

We didn't want her to be there all night either, so we got on with masking, splurging and cleaning up. Within half an hour our track was in the correct place again. Only time would tell if it would stay there.

As Mum left, a minibus of people arrived. Seb's

friend, Fer, had come all the way from mainland Spain to celebrate this first night with us and he wasn't the sort to drive around with empty seats in his van.

Just to show everyone how well prepared we were, we had strung our hammocks between two sun-umbrellas. We thought they would come in useful as a few people didn't have anything to sleep in, and anyway we'd promised ourselves we'd get them up at least once.

Although we've never used them properly, they've always seemed very Bear Grylls. They have integral mosquito nets which zip around the occupant, so I decided to demonstrate this impressive bedding to the captive audience. Once I was properly installed, Fer insisted he help me into the mosquito net and zip me in. Unfortunately, once closed, the zip then jammed and I was trapped inside my own hammock. All my friends were then exceedingly helpful, aiding me with violent swinging and additional tickling. Only Fer desisted and that was just beause he felt guilty. After five minutes of performing an intense wrestling match with the net and my friends, the pathetically flimsy zip broke completely.

"You'll have to rip it …"

"Or stay there forever …"

People were so helpful! I ripped.

There was a large bush at the back of the beach which was alive with little brown birds. One of them was on the ground fluttering like a chicken. It was clearly very young. I picked it up and put it safely in the bush before walking back towards the sea where the others had made a big circle of tents, sunbeds and sleeping bags all surrounded by candles which we would light when darkness finally arrived.

Five minutes later the bird appeared beside me

and began hopping round the circle. It must have taken considerable effort to hop so far, but he was fearless, so we called him Freddy.

Nick with Freddy

We began to play with him. First we put him on Sandra's head, but she didn't appreciate it and we were worried that her high pitched scream of: "Get it off! Get it off!" might upset Freddy's feelings. So I put him on my shoulder and he instantly showed how comfortable he was by poo-ing on me. We put him back in the bush at least five times, but he kept returning and being sociable even though we never fed him.

Freddy was happy. We were happy. Only the very best of our friends had arrived at the beach, there were no Guardia Civil, and we finally felt as if our adventure had begun. However, we were still knackered and at an embarrassingly early hour we crawled into our tent while the rest of them were still chatting and laughing in their circle of flickering candle light.

Day Two

Nick: Li-los made all the difference, we slept well and when the sun rose we were fully refreshed. I had worried that the plastic would make us sweat, but with a sleeping bag on top, it was fine. Li-los were our only possible option as there is no space in Rocky for the padded mats most campers use, so we were relieved that they worked.

Unfortunately Little Alice and Jade had only brought a sarong to sleep underneath and they spent the night shivering and uncomfortable. When we emerged from our tent they were willing time to speed up so they could catch the first bus back to Palma and get some rest.

By the time we gathered for breakfast, Freddy was already hopping between everyone's legs, so I put him back on my shoulder to keep him safe.

I made a quick call to Dad to check the forecast, because we had promised we would phone before setting out each day, even though the weather looked fair. After we had collected two large bags of rubbish from around the beach and put them beside the bins, we decided to leave even though it was only just after eight o'clock and there wasn't a breath of wind.

We had got into a routine of paddling out to get away from any obstacles before we began to hoist sail. Sailing directly off slipways and beaches is unnecessarily stressy and we weren't in a rush. However, our friend Pep disagreed.

He's a regatta sailor and definitely knows more than both of us put together, but we were happy going at our own pace. Pep was completely convinced that the only way to exit was with full sail up, straight for the entrance, with or without wind. He was voicing his opinions very strongly; you could even say he was being a total control freak. Having tried reasoning, and then detailed explanations, we gave up and brokered a compromise by letting him put the jib up. Even then, he put so much tension on the halyard that the stay wasn't doing anything. We had to quietly slacken it off directly we got round the corner.

Freddy was back in his bush, and with an energetic push from Alice, we were floating on a millpond bay, paddling past anchored yachts towards the entrance. The jib hung uselessly; off on the horizon we could see the dark shape of the island of Cabrera, the archipelago's most important marine reserve and a national wildlife park. I dreamt of seeing impressive megafauna today. Sperm whales, leatherback turtles and large pods of dolphins were all creatures that had swum alongside us during my fantasy hours. Surely today would be the day.

When the wind arrived we thought about trying a few tacks to see how our repair held up, then decided it was way too scary and continued using the foot-strap for a further twenty-four hours.

There was less rubbish in the sea today, except around Sa Rapita which was grim. We had intended to stop for the night at Es Caragol but when we arrived it was far too crowded for us to approach the beach.

"Do you think we'll make it as far as Cala Llombards tonight if we keep going?" I asked Seb. It was a conundrum as the wind was light and slightly against us, but we thought it might be fresher around the next headland.

"It's a gamble," Seb replied. "It will be a hell of a long paddle if we're wrong, but I don't see how we can land here without upsetting a lot of people."

We decided to go for it and shortly afterwards Seb announced he could feel a siesta overtaking him. Almost as soon as his hat covered his eyes, his breathing slowed and I knew he was completely out of it. Seb is a genius at power napping – anywhere, anytime, any position, no problem! His favoured chill-out spot throughout the trip was lying along the narrow strip of hull with his head wedged on the cockpit lip. To any normal person this would have been a form of torture, but he would sleep there like a babe in arms for hours.

I was enjoying a gentle drift in the peaceful afternoon. We were quite far off-shore, but I didn't see this as a problem as I was convinced we were going so slowly that I had hours in which to manoeuvre Rocky in towards the shoreline. Suddenly, I saw what I thought was Cala Santanyi. This catapulted me straight out of my tranquil daydream. If it was Santanyi then we were moving far faster than I had calculated. Our wake didn't seem at all impressive, but the wind had veered behind us and it was just possible that we were several miles further on than I had believed, and, if so, we could easily overshoot Cala Llombards very, very soon.

"Dude!"

I'm not sure if the shout or my kick roused Seb, but in an instant he was fully awake and we were bent over our charts.

"I'm not totally sure, let's find the GPS." We hadn't thought we would need this, so it took a fair amount of rummaging to locate it. There was no doubt, we needed to turn for land.

The moment we did so, the wind died. Totally. Forty-five minutes of strenuous paddling later, we could see the detail of Cala Llombards' white sands, or we would have been able to if every square centimetre hadn't been covered in brightly coloured sun-umbrellas.

"Oh my god, it's busier than Es Caragol, what are we going to do?" A small whine may have entered my voice at this point, my arms were dropping off, my mouth was like two pieces of sandpaper and my legs felt as if they had been folded into a crouch for days.

"Let's head for the left side and try to slot in behind those rocks," Seb suggested. By now I was no more than a grumpy auto-paddler, we squeezed Rocky's nose onto a tiny triangle of beach and gave it a bit of a shove. The rest would have to wait.

Seb: The entrance to Cala Llobards is camouflaged by a pair of rocky, pine-covered outcrops. A few small green-doored boat houses and mini dwellings are scattered on the right side as you sail in, while the beach at the end is deeper than it is wide. About mid-way down the perfect sand (which you can appreciate when the bodies have moved so you can actually see it), there is a wooden building with a rush roof and four or five bar stools in front of a wooden counter. There are also some bright green parrots which are encouraged back onto their perches when they become too adventurous and leave the bar in search of beach action. The road leads right down to the sand and parking is free, no wonder there were loads of people.

The minute we landed Nick stretched himself out on the sand and slept. He was so wiped out he'd only moved a couple of paces from Rocky before taking on the appearance of a slightly wind-burnt corpse. We were both pretty disappointed that we'd sailed for two full days and had not seen anything we could put on our megafauna sheets for Ondine. The growing concern that the Mediterranean sea is becoming a watery desert could be a valid one.

I called Mum and she said she wanted to drive over and bring us some tuna pasta, so I didn't do too much damage to our ship's stores – apart from the water.

There are porta-potties on this beach which smelt horrific, but to us they were a real luxury. When Mum arrived we were able to lure her towards the parrots which led to her agreeing to buy us all cold Cokes. At the risk of sounding like a TV advert, the taste of an ice cold Coke, after days of warm water out of plastic containers, is close to orgasmic. Yes, I'm afraid I did the whole bit of pressing the cool slippery glass against my face before taking great gulps that froze my chest and stomach on the way down. That Coke was truly memorable!

The lady at the bar seemed cool. After Mum had left we watched her shut up shop and bring the parrots inside. As the sun left the inlet, families with children abandoned the beach and small groups of friends took their place. We put up our tent and pulled the boat further up the sand to keep her safe. There was a party of ladies who all went swimming, except for one who stayed sitting on the rocks beside Rocky. She was English and when she heard us talking she asked us to explain what we were doing. When her friends finally emerged from the water, she got us to tell them too. One of the ladies, named Marita, owned a local supermarket and she immediately invited us to call at the shop tomorrow morning for a free breakfast.

To say we were delighted would be a big understatement; we couldn't wipe the grins off our faces if we tried. It wasn't just about the food – well, it may have been in Nick's case – but for me it was amazing that so many people who didn't know us had been so kind to a couple of scruffy teenagers. While we were around Palma, we were often looking OK in school uniform, or the people concerned knew our parents, but we really didn't expect this level of generosity from total strangers. It may sound like a cliché by this stage, but Marita was another example that our island is stuffed full of very, very nice people!

After the ladies had given us directions for the morning and left, I made a final trip to the porta-potties. I was just about to wander back to the tent when a big Land rover sped past me and across the sand, skidding to a halt in front of the bar. A tanned giant sprang from the driver's seat, biceps bulging above a perfectly ripped six-pack, naked, apart from a mini pair of shorts. In a couple of mighty strides he was at the passenger side of the 4 x 4. Given his appearance, I expected him to emerge from behind the door with a Tarzan rope slung around him, or a stack of full beer barrels balanced on one little finger, yet as I edged passed him, in the most inconspicuous way I could muster, he emerged cradling a ridiculously cute Chihuahua. Two big globe eyes were topped with a pair of over-sized ears on a seriously undersized body. The furry companion for this man should have been a Pit bull, or if he was letting his feminine side have a real airing, a German Shepherd, but definitely, never, ever, this! Yet this miniature man's best friend accompanied Hercules into the bar.

To give it credit, the protective Chihuahua barked a great deal throughout the night. Whether our tent was making it extra nervous, I don't know, but we hoped that its master and the bar lady weren't as cold, inside the bar, as we were outside. Although the day had been scorching, the night time temperature plummeted and our abiding memory of our night at Cala Llombards is of being completely chilled to the bone, in the middle of July, in Mallorca. Weird!

Day Three

Seb: The sun woke us early and after the cold and blustery night, it was a relief to stretch and feel ourselves being gently thawed out. We began cleaning the beach as it was far too early to head for Marita's shop. We were being pretty leisurely about our task as we had at least a couple of hours to kill. Eventually a German lady and her friend came down for a swim and saw Pete's QR codes, so, after we'd explained what we were up to, they photographed the signs and promised to begin following the blog.

Sometime into our second bag of rubbish, Hercules emerged from the bar with his tiny companion and the bar owner put out her parrots.

"What are you two up to?" she asked. "You're doing my job, I could have stayed in bed!"

When we told her about Ondine and Mediterranea, she was great.

"Come over for a drink when you've finished, I owe you one."

We were soon sitting in front of two cold Cokes. The day was beginning very well indeed.

As we sat sipping our drinks, she told us how the bar had to be guarded every night because she'd suffered a series of break-ins. The bar itself was a fairly flimsy wooden hut, so I reckoned that, if the Chihuahua had not been there, it would have been quite easy for any thief to enter and remove most of the contents.

I'm not quite sure how it happened, but we agreed that I would go and find Marita's supermarket while Nick stayed with Rocky and packed up the tent. It was a beautiful morning to be going in search of breakfast and I had no difficulty finding the shop.

Inside there were two people serving, but neither was Marita. I asked if the owner was around.

"No, más tarde." (later)

Seb with Marita in front of her shop.

Although "later" is a very flexible concept in Spain and can mean anything from five minutes to several days, I wasn't bothered, I could feel it in my bones that today was going to be good.

I sat down on the pavement outside and waited. After twenty minutes a scooter skidded round the corner and Marita jumped off, all smiles and enthusiasm. Instantly she became a human dynamo, talking constantly while grabbing food off shelves, making sandwiches and stuffing everything into big bags. The longer it went on, the more I couldn't believe this was all for just the two of us. With a final flourish she presented me with three bulging bags and five litres of water, before running over to the till and taking out a 10 euro note.

"For your charity," she said in Spanish.

I hardly knew how to adequately thank her. We had met for a few minutes on a beach the night before, yet she had done all of this for a pair of "guiris" (pale-skinned foreigners). I was humbled by her generosity.

By the time I got to Rocky my hands were aching as the bags and water sliced into my fingers. The journey back seemed considerably longer than when I was out-bound.

"Oh my God, Dude! I thought you'd just have a couple of out-of-date sandwiches and some over-ripe fruit!"

"Nope, she gave us the absolute best, and on top of that she's sponsored us!"

"Wow, that's incredible"

At that moment an English lady came over to us.

"I've heard about what you're doing," opening her handbag, she pulled out another 10 euro note, "this is for your charity."

We could hardly believe our ears, or our eyes! Before we'd had our first bite of the morning, we'd raised an additional 20 euros for Mediterranea, and we had enough supplies to last us for days. We settled into a hearty breakfast, worthy of our English roots.

"I called Dad for a forecast," Nick mumbled through mouthfuls. "He said Capella's heading for Cala Mitjana and if we get there they'll give us a meal and a shower."

"That would be good. If we know we can have a shower we can swim before we set out."

"It's not very far on the chart, but we've done OK so far. I guess it doesn't matter if we give ourselves an easier day, if you don't mind," Nick said.

I thought it would be great, we could do plenty of hard sailing later on in the trip. However, by the time we left Cala Llombards the wind had strengthened and the sea was already choppy. We were forced to beat the entire way and all parts of the rig were fully tested by the time we saw the entrance to the bay. Nothing broke, but we were both covered in dried salt, so the promise of a fresh shower was something to be luxuriated in.

Inside the bay were a collection of small yachts and llauts, so, with no sign of MY Capella we beached Rocky and enjoyed a long swim before making headway into Marita's second bag. Today we could eat as much as we liked. We knew we'd get fed tonight. Brilliant!

Nick: A massive shadow began to spread across the bay, it was so extensive that our eyes were forced open from our après-lunch doze. Capella had arrived.

"There's no way they'll manage to anchor her in here, there's no room!" Seb said in a tone that echoed my own rising fears that this would be as close as we would get to Dad and the promised shower.

"He's going to have to turn round and go somewhere else."

The day had been magnificent so far, but it didn't look set to last.

"Is he going to try and get into that tiny gap?" Seb asked a few minutes later, as the hum of bow-thrusters reverberated around the small bay and Capella began to spin in her own pool of water.

"Surely not!"

I looked up at the bridge and saw Tommy on the wheel. Tommy Blohm is joint owner of Capella with his parents. The family own and run the Harry Bread bakeries that operate throughout Germany and export all over the world. Although I had been told Tommy was an experienced skipper, I didn't expect the level of awesome manoeuvring that was going on.

"He's good!" I said to Seb.

"Bloody impressive!" Seb replied, "They might actually manage it."

Rocky moored alongside MY Capella.

Suddenly there was a gigantic anchor splash, and a uniformed man raced to the stern of the floating leviathan. Leaping from the gangplank, I recognised Dad: he who constantly complains about his bad back, achy shoulder and various other age-related ailments.

Before my disbelieving eyes he had morphed into a monkey. Dancing across the slippery rocks he had a bowline tied off in a millisecond and was back aboard trimming anchor and lines while a smiling Tommy cracked open a beer.

"I never thought I'd call Dad 'agile'!"

"That was the giraffe's horns and the elephant's trunk!" Seb was clearly as surprised as me.

We'd been using these phrases ever since Dad's predictive text had labelled us the "rat's whiskers" a few days previously.

Capella was moored, and Andrea, Tommy's wife, was beckoning us over, while little Charlotta and Carla were dashing around the deck squealing with excitement as newly-agile-Dad lowered a couple of fenders for us to tie up against.

Tommy, Andrea and the children couldn't have been more welcoming to a couple of grubby teenage boys. I have no idea how Dad persuaded them they wanted to allow him to bring his family to work, but we were given five star treatment, and everybody was constantly smiling. After we had met everyone and been given cold drinks, we were allowed to drive the RIB around and generally play with all of Capella's "toys". It was heaven. Here we were, meant to be roughing it in the name of charity, yet invited onto a multi-million euro yacht and treated like proper guests! It doesn't get better than that!

Ali, the chef, kept up an endless supply of irresistible goodies and we had no doubt that our combined additional weight was going to make Rocky float lower in the water tomorrow. Eventually we began making tentative noises about pitching our tent before it got dark.

"No, no," Andrea exclaimed, "You can sleep in the saloon ... once you've showered."

We didn't need telling twice, and were soon looking almost neat, having broken out our sole clean T-shirts in honour of dinner.

Throughout the evening we played constantly with Charlotta and Carla. It didn't seem to matter that we couldn't understand a word they said. We just kept nodding and smiling; smiling and nodding, with the odd head pat thrown in. It seemed to be the right response.

When we finally said "good night" to them we discovered the saloon had been made up with crisply laundered, snow white sheets. One of us would be on the sofa, the other on an airbed, so we decided to do "Paper, Scissors, Stone" to see who got the bed. After four attempts Seb looked at me in disbelief.

"You have the bed!" he said in exasperation, "I'm never playing that with you again, we think too alike!"
I lay down in deep spongy comfort, a pristine pillow beneath my head. I reckon the grin stayed on my face all night long.

White sheets!

Day Four

Nick: The day filtered through smear-less windows onto our pristine shrouded bodies. The air conditioning purred softly, allowing me to snuggle deeper into the padded indulgence of my bed and ignore the clear blue sky and burning sun that was already climbing well above the horizon. This level of luxury was in danger of clouding any urgency I might have had to get under way.

I heard Seb turn over, and suspected that he, too, was doing his utmost to convince himself we could lie around for a couple more hours. Twenty minutes later, the appearance of Charlotta and Carla racing round the decks dragged us out. Exiting our quality controlled atmosphere, the heat bounded over us the moment we opened the door. It was going to be a scorching day.

With the air this fiery, there would definitely be wind, but unfortunately it was forecast to be dead against us. We needed to get going, we were in for a hard sail.

After a breakfast that should have lasted us through to dinner time, Ali pressed a bag of food onto us and we got ready to climb down into Rocky and cast off.

Carla tugged at my T-shirt. I looked down to see her big eyes looking up at me; a small hand was outstretched holding a bright pink plastic gem. She looked slightly coy, so I did my usual thing of smiling and nodding. This provoked a stream of excited German, so I smiled some more and made some "ahha" and "ooh, umm" noises as it seemed as if a little more input was required.

She smiled and rattled off another

incomprehensible paragraph. It looked as if I would have to go for the full smile, nod, ahha, and head pat all at the same time, which I dutifully did.

She thrust the florescent pink jewel up towards me so, with the nod, I said, "Yes, it's very beautiful."

By this time Seb was already in Rocky. Carla seemed to want me to appreciate the item more, so I knelt down to give it closer attention as she pushed it under my nose.

"Yes, it's really lovely, but it's yours, you must keep it," I tried, grinning away and nodding until I was perilously close to dizziness.

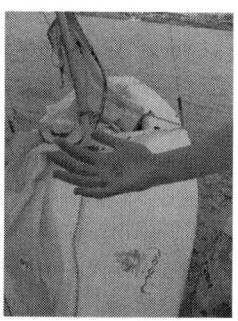

Carla's gem – my good luck charm.

She laughed at me and grabbed my hand. Opening out my fingers, she pressed her treasure into my palm before folding my fingers back round it again. She was my absolute favourite little kid ever! Now I understood. I told her how grateful I was and how I was sure it would bring us luck and loads of other things in English which she didn't understand, so she smiled, nodded, said ahha, and patted me on the head. As I got off my knees and climbed down to Rocky, I was quite choked up by this five-year-old's generosity.

Dad cast us off and everyone was waving as we

broke out the paddles to get away from Capella's immaculate paintwork before we got the sails up, but my smile was for Carla who had given me my good luck charm. I was so happy that she'd liked me after all the nodding and smiling. I put the precious plastic piece into the secure change pocket of my swimming trunks and vowed to never lose it. As I pulled up the jib I was overwhelmed by the warm fuzzy feeling.

The water in the bay was crystal clear and we were able to watch Rocky's shadow moving across the sand beneath us. However, once we rounded the entrance we were hit by a short choppy swell plus the full force of a strengthening wind against us.

With all the comfy beds, good food and welcoming people, plus the familiarity of having Dad around, I was feeling sluggishly content, so it wasn't until the first wave landed on me that I realised I was going to need to snap out of it and concentrate on some serious sailing. After a couple more doses of cold water, I was brutally back to business, but it took me a further half an hour to really wake up and enjoy the ride Rocky was giving us. There was plenty of green water coming over the bow and we were having to make full use of the foot straps and lean out as far as possible to keep her upright.

It was an unpleasant truth that we were surfing past a considerable amount of rubbish; there was too much, and we were pressed too hard, for us to record all of it on the sheets Brad had given us. We were now four days out and, still, we had not seen a single dolphin or any other creature that could come anywhere near the category of "megafauna".

When I wasn't helming there was more time to stare across the waves and think. I had my favourite spot for chilling, right at the bow with my legs either side of the jib stay. Occasionally the jib would give a bit of shade and I could spend hours looking at the wide expanse of sea all around us. I remembered all the dolphin stories Mum and Dad told of when they used to run a charter boat round the Balearic Islands, of how pods of them would play in the bow wave; of accidentally hitting a sleepy basking shark while trying to avoid its friend; of leatherback turtles ambling their way through the waters; yet twenty years later we saw nothing. Brad's passion to regenerate the underwater world was certainly needed, but it seemed to me there was a mountain of work to do before the marine environment could be branded "healthy" again.

Seb: I was blasted out of an hypnotic state by a green glass-bottomed boat that appeared behind us at speed and then gave two friendly "parps" on his air horn. Looking up sharply, we saw the decks crowded with tourists who were waving at us and taking photos, so we waved back like complete lunatics, which made them wave even more – especially the kids. It was great. The captain slowed down to allow for more waving and photo-taking, before giving us two more hoots and steaming along the coastline. It wasn't a dolphin, but it was nice.

As we drew level with the entrance to Porto Cristo we decided to check the chart coordinates against out GPS reading. The idea was to reassure ourselves about how accurate the GPS was and how, if we ever had to use our PLBs in anger, rescue services would be able to find us in minutes - it was a rough day and the wind kept increasing, so it was natural to start thinking about these things.

"Are you sure you're reading it right?" I asked Nick when he gave me the latitude and longitude off the chart. It didn't match my gadget by a difference of more than four miles. We swapped.

"OK, let's try not to get into trouble," Nick concluded after we had checked and rechecked the coordinates, "I think we can safely say we may have to rely on swimming in a crisis. Perhaps we should ease off the wind a bit."

The "easing" didn't last long though; it was hard enough making headway with the wind dead against us as it was. Permanent easing wasn't really an option.

After five and a half hours, salt encrusted, and feeling as if we'd been through a sand blaster, we turned into the narrow inlet of Cala Petita. Guide books will tell you that Cala Petita is a protected area of virgin beach with clear waters favoured by nudists, so we thought it was a good place to spend the night.

The beach is no more than twenty metres wide at the end of a long channel that curves round to the right at the point where there is a large rock which looks as if it is precariously balanced on top of another one and will fall at any minute. A rough track through scrub-covered rocks leads down to the sand. It was filthy.

There wasn't even enough clean space to pitch our minute tent. The last few stragglers were packing up their picnic baskets, so we quickly collared a couple of guys to help us haul Rocky a little further up the beach, then we set to work with our rubbish bags.

We still hadn't seen any megafauna and Cala Petita seemed to be an illustration of the reason why. Unlike the major tourist beaches which are regularly cleaned, the small ones we were pulling into rely on people taking their own rubbish home with them, plus, preferably, anything else that has been washed up in the last storm. There were old cans, bottles, plastic bags and a volleyball, plus the usual indecipherable jumble gracing the waterline. After twenty minutes we had a clear-ish area for our camp. We would tackle the rest in the morning.

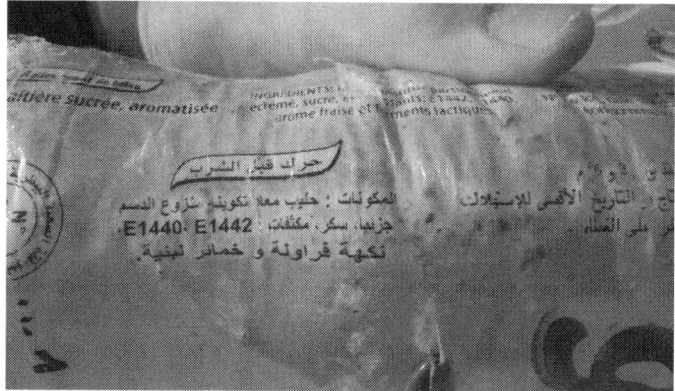

We found plenty of rubbish with Arabic writing on it.

Today felt really long. I ached everywhere and once I had drunk my fill of water, I could hardly be bothered to scrabble around in the dry bag to see what we had left to eat. By now the cala was completely silent. I knew the stars would look amazing. There were no street lamps in sight to obscure the view, but there was also no way I would be awake after dusk. By the time we had emptied a few cans of beans, tuna and pineapple down us, we were both ready for bed. We've given up making predictions about where we're heading for each day as we never manage to get it right. Tomorrow, we'll just sail on and see where we end up.

Day Five

Seb: We slept solidly until the sun woke us up just before 6am. We've swapped li-los so I'm on the Sponge Bob Square Pants one and Nick's taken over Spiderman because the separate pillow on Sponge Bob got a puncture and Nick's too tall for more than half of him to remain on the rest of it so it made sense to change over. We thought of using our clothing to fill in the pillow space, but they're not the sorts of things you want by your nose throughout the night. Even pillow less, Sponge Bob still has his attractions; he's wider and deeper than Spiderman.

We completely filled three large rubbish bags with the rest of the debris on the beach.

"Now what should we do with them? If we leave them here they'll end up being blown out to sea."

Nick scampered to the top of the rocks, eager to

provide me with an answer. "There's a village over there," he announced. "There's bound to be a bin just over that hill, it can't be more than fifteen minutes' walk away."

Suddenly the ties on the three bags were cutting into my hands and Nick had wedged the volleyball under my left arm and was enthusiastically clapping me on the back.

"Off you go mate, I'll start getting Rocky ready to sail."

I blame minor exhaustion for the fact that I didn't consider the fact that Nick's sole functioning eye isn't a reliable judge of distance. The bushes tore at my bare legs and the plastic bags stuck themselves to any part they brushed against, as I sweated my way over hillock after hillock in my quest for the elusive bin. What with Marita's shop and then this, our journey seemed to be as much about long distance bag carrying as sailing.

Over an hour later I staggered back onto the beach hoping Nick hadn't already packed away all the water.

"Hey Dude! Where have you been? Did you meet people?" Nick said, grinning up at me happily from his horizontal position on the sand.

"Not a soul," I growled, grabbing the water bottle. "...and, no, there isn't a bin the other side of the hill, and it's definitely not a fifteen minute walk!"

"Sorry mate!"

He did have the courtesy to look sheepish as we paddled out of the cala. The people on an anchored boat called out to us as we went passed and asked what the stickers on our hull were about, so we stopped for a drift and a chat. They offered us food and water, which was really kind, but we still had quite a bit left from

Capella, so we declined and paddled on to the entrance to hoist sail.

There was a good wind and Nick had Rocky moving well on a beam reach, so I decided to grab a siesta after my morning's trek. I'm pretty good at napping anywhere and had enjoyed some excellent Z-eds even in the confines of this tiny dinghy.

I woke up feeling great, but slightly disorientated, something had changed.

Rocky was practically at a standstill, there wasn't even a whisper of wind. It was difficult to see where the sea ended and the sky began, they were welded together into one endless, flat expanse of pure deep blue. God, it was hot.

We took it in turns to cool down and have a swim, we even tried towing Rocky for a bit. There was no way we were going to get around the island like this. Even when each of us were towing with all our might, and felt sure we were ploughing through the water, we appeared static against the land. We paddled, we towed, we ate and drank, we wiggled the tiller and whistled for wind. In reality, we bobbed. For hours.

Late in the afternoon the wind began creeping back and we inched closer to the shore. When Capdepera lighthouse hove into view we decided to head for Cala Agulla for the night and thank the wind god that we'd made it that far.

Nick: Cala Agulla has a long crescent of immaculately clean, golden sand backed by a few dunes and a house on the right-hand edge of the arc. The building is in a place where no private building is meant to be on this island, yet many times we have seen houses like this, right on the beach, in positions that must be worth a fortune. There was one in Cala Mitjana too.

We pulled Rocky up just below the house, well out of the way of the pedaloes and swimmers that were all over the rest of the beach. I had phoned Mum to tell her where we were and Chris was driving her over with food and fresh contact lenses. It would be Chris's first time driving since he'd passed his test and I wondered if Mum would arrive in a nervous state. In Spain you're not allowed to drive without a qualified instructor until you've passed your test, so this would be the first time Mum had experienced Chris's newly developed skill.

I went to buy two bottles of cold water. It was a luxury, but all our water had been baking in the sun the entire day and we were dreaming of drinking something cool. I noticed a shower being used at the far end of the beach but didn't investigate because I wanted to get back to Seb whilst the water was still dripping with condensation down the sides. When I told Seb of my discovery, he downed his water so quickly it froze his stomach, and then began jogging down the wide swaithe of sand.

Back at Rocky I idly watched the people who were milling around the house. For some bizarre reason the large windows that would have looked out over the sea were boarded up, yet there were a couple of vans there, and plenty of activity, it was definitely in use. I wondered if it had been invaded by squatters.

Half an hour later Seb returned. He was not the happy bunny I had been expecting.

"Bloody hell! Those showers are salt water. All I've achieved is to get boiling hot again and have a half hour walk because this beach is so bloody long!"

I decided it was probably best to stay very quiet

and hope that our food parcel arrived soon.

It's easy to spot Chris's bright red hair at a distance, so we knew well in advance that Mum had gone to the wrong end of the beach as the two figures approached laden down with bags.

Mum didn't look too bad, and even said Chris had the makings of a good driver. Chris, naturally, had to beat me up a bit before helping us to pull Rocky further up the beach. I can't pretend that I don't enjoy the fact that I'm already far taller than he's ever going to be, but I do have to pay for it occasionally!

However, nothing was going to get in the way of the hot food Mum had brought with her, so we sent Chris off with a camera to take moody sunset shots, and got stuck into some serious eating. Once we literally could not move, we began to think of other things.

"Did you bring some more contact lenses?"

"Yes," Mum replied, pulling out two boxes and giving one to each of us.

"Did you bring the other box as well?" Seb asked tentatively.

"I thought I'd bring it when you ran out of this box."

"Umm, no, you see, unlike Nick, I have two eyes. You've brought the lenses for my left eye, the other box is for the right one."

Poor Mum, she looked completely shocked. She generally checks absolutely everything before setting off anywhere and, as usual, she had lugged a load of extra things across the sand which we didn't need at all, just in case we did. But this vital object she'd deliberately left back in the kitchen in Palma.

"Oh god, you can't both be Cyclopes! How many days' supply have you got left?" It had been an hour's drive to get to us, there was no way she was going to do it again tonight.

"I've got a couple more days, and I can use my glasses if I run out," Seb said, trying to make her feel better.

The people around the house were looking over at us and pointing at our tent. I hoped we weren't going to encounter our first problems about camping on the beach, which is technically illegal. They didn't look like plain-clothed policemen, so I hoped they weren't going to make any unnecessary phone calls.

The mosquitos arrived in droves directly the sun dipped below the horizon, so as Mum and Chris's backs staggered away from us, burdened by far lighter picnic bags, we raced to zip ourselves in under canvas and hoped to avoid trouble from the house by staying very, very quiet.

I woke once during the night when rain began pummeling the tent. I tried to wriggle away from the sides so I would keep dry, but it was no good, the tent was too small, wherever either of us moved we couldn't avoid having contact with some piece of wall, and soon the drumming of the droplets sent me back to sleep. It wasn't as if it was cold.

It wasn't the biggest two-man tent!

Day Six

Nick: Someone was shaking me.
"Duuuude! There's something weird going on."
"Err. Wot?"
"Get your one eye out of bed and look at this!"

My head joined Seb's in the tent entrance. We must have looked like a frantic two-headed tortoise as we snapped our heads back and forth to take in our surroundings. It was around 6.30am but the beach we had zipped away last night had been transformed by reams of tape. Dozens of official-looking people in bright yellow jackets were scurrying around. A couple of them were talking and waving their arms at the hippies who were camped a hundred metres further down the sand.

"What the hell's going on?"
"Dunno, but I reckon we're going to be asked to move."
"How can we?" I replied. The sea was a study in serenity, there was not a single ripple, not the slightest hint of wind. We could not expect a ghost of a breeze for hours. The rain last night had washed the dust from the sky, it was a spectacular morning.

We pulled our heads back into the tent.
"Maybe if we keep very quiet they'll leave us alone," Seb said. "The hippies probably argued with them or something."
"Let's drag in the food bag and have breakfast in case they make us go."

Seb stuck his head and arm out, and then froze.
"Bloody hell!"

My head joined his and looked right. A man with a massive camera was walking towards us, followed by three others carrying arc lamps and a huge reflective sheet.

We were in the middle of a film set.

"God knows why they need more light in Mallorca!" Seb said as he stretched for the food bag and attempted to avoid eye contact with any of the scurriers, while he dragged it back into our lair.

We munched self-consciously. Even inside the tent we were very aware of the number of yellow jackets and cameras that surrounded us, it was quite intimidating.

"We can't leave, but perhaps we should pack everything into Rocky so it looks a bit neater," I said when we'd finished.

As we began our normal routine of getting everything stowed away, one of the yellow jackets passed very close to us.

"Do you need us to move?" I asked.

"If they haven't told you to, don't worry," he replied while waving in the direction of a gaggle of clearly important people, because two of them had chairs.

"What are you filming?" I asked. He didn't look hugely busy so I thought he might chat.

"It's a film about a writer and in this scene he's writing his book in Jamaica, only the company couldn't afford to go on location there, so we're here instead. The writer's meant to be in a first floor room, that's why those guys are holding palm fronds in front of the windows, so it looks as if the room's high up."

We had been wondering what the palm holders were up to. Now the boarded up bits of the house began to make sense. The garden area in front sported a lush carpet of fake grass and a number of plastic pot plants. From the outside the whole thing looked careless and messy, but no doubt the film would be cut to get rid of people running around with large branches, acres of "keep out" tape, and plastic horticulture.

"Who owns this place?" I asked, not really expecting my friendly yellow jacket to know.

"Señor March. He also owns Cala Caragol and Cala Mitjana, his grandparents were drug traffickers."

I knew the March family, who own the respected Banca March, had some fairly shady dealings during Franco's time, but I'd not heard anything about drugs before. However, my source was undoubtedly Mallorquin to the bone, so maybe he had inside information, or perhaps it was a tall tale.

Suddenly he was called to join the scurrying again. Things were becoming very hectic around our little patch. A speaker horn squeaked into life, followed by a booming voice, "Right everybody, quiet ... ACTION!"

There was no option, we had to get out the oars.

Seb: As silently as possible we slid Rocky into the water, pushing her with exaggerated slowness to make as few splashes as possible. We did ballerina impressions to vault over the sides with soundless grace. Dipping our paddles in a stealthy unison that would be envied by the SAS, we made our escape from Mollywood. Then we bobbed off-shore, with absolutely no wind at all.

There was no point in putting up the sails, and paddling wouldn't achieve much when the wind would probably come up in an hour or so. Nick began practicing bowlines on the main sheet.

"Why is it that when I don't need a bowline I can tie them with no problem at all, but the minute they're vital they just disintegrate on me?"

Nick has had a problem with bowlines ever since we started this venture. Sit him down in a room with a piece of string and they come out perfect every time, but when you really need a bomb-proof loop on the end of a rope, Nick's not your man!

"Dunno Dude, I guess it's just something you're crap at."

"Thanks Man. At least we're not both crap at the same things, that would be bad."

"Except knowing if it's our right of way, we're both completely crap at that."

"True, but don't tell Dad, he'd get freaky about that one. Anyway, as we're small and under sail I reckon we have right of way over pretty well everything."

"I'm not sure size comes into it, but you're right. We just have to avoid meeting any other sailing boats who might expect us to know."

"Exactly!"

It was great the way Nick and I could always agree on problem solving.

The wind eventually arrived and by mid-afternoon we had decided to stop at Playa del Coll Baix which is just below the tip of the headland that leads round into the Bay of Pollensa. If there is no change in the weather tomorrow and we are able to sail, we will definitely pass the half-way mark, which is pretty exciting. However, we are now at the end of Day Six and we still have not seen even a splash of megafauna. That is a massive disappointment.

Playa del Coll Baix is a long fringe of beach backed by towering clay cliffs. Naturally there's no mobile coverage at sea level, so after we'd got help hauling Rocky out, we walked up the path until we got a signal and were able to send our position to our parents. This taught us two things: first, we're on another nudist beach and people are beginning to question our route-planning criteria; secondly it's a five kilometre walk over crumbling cliff paths to get from the nearest parking spot to the beach so there'll be no way we're getting any food or contact lenses for my right eye tonight. Still, the place is stunning.

From half way up the cliff I took a photo of Rocky. She came out as the speck next to a pine tree branch that was about twenty metres below me. Tomorrow I intend to climb to the top and see what the view is like from there. It should be awesome.

This was the view from half way up the cliff at Playa del Coll Baix. Rocky is the tiny white dot to the right of the pine tree branch.

Day Seven

Seb: The morning was completely still. It seemed to hang motionless preparing itself for the arrival of the heat.

It was time to climb. I looked up at the wall in front of me, it was challenging me. I'd never done any climbing before, but how hard could it be?

I kicked off my flip-flops at the base of the cliff, conscious that they would get in the way and aware there was a possibility I could need my toes to cling on with during the tricky bits.

I considered taking the path, but decided against following it. The crumbly track appeared to wind around a lot and take an awful long route to go upwards, which seemed like a waste of time when I could go straight.

The first bit was OK. Definitely a bit of an adrenaline rush, but I was enjoying working out where my next hand hold could be and manoeuvring my body flat against the face like a lizard. I had been cramped up inside a small dinghy and a tiny tent for many hours every day, so I enjoyed going on long walks and exploring whenever I could.

After about thirty metres the cliff seemed to become steeper, there were rocks overhanging which were hard to inch around. I grabbed for one and it pulled out in my hand, bouncing down to the bottom and exploding at the base into a shower of minute pieces.

I was beginning to feel worried. In my eagerness to leave, I'd forgotten to drink water beforehand and my mouth already tasted like a butcher's armpit. I looked down. Returning that way didn't seem to be an option, pushing upwards with my feet had made much of it into a slide, I could only keep going up and hope that I met up with the path at the top.

After the third rock pulled out and bounced away from me, I could no longer hear the sound when it finally hit the bottom. I vowed to stop looking down as it wasn't doing me any good. My stomach was in so many knots it was a small ball of pain beneath my sternum. My arms were shaking with the effort of lifting my weight, yet every time I committed to a new hand hold I was sickened with fear that it would suddenly tear itself from the cliff, taking me down with it. This was not the best idea I'd ever had.

Covered in mud and with every one of my limbs trembling with exhaustion, I slithered over the top, half an hour later. I lay flat on my back. For a while I was certain that if I stood and looked out at the sea, dizziness would overcome me and I would topple off the pinnacle of safety I'd finally reached.

Consciously slowing my breathing, I rolled landwards into a sitting position and began to survey where I was. It wasn't good.

I was now marooned on top of something very tall. There was no way of getting to the elusive path, wherever that eventually hit civilization. If anything I was worse off than I had been at any other stage. The only option was down, and it looked likely that my descent could be far faster than I wanted it to be.

I couldn't even identify Rocky from this height let alone see Nick.

With the amount of mud on me I definitely blended in perfectly with my surroundings. I was seriously, seriously scared and I knew, absolutely, that I had very good reason for thinking we might not complete our trip round the island after all.

Nick: I didn't take much notice when Seb announced he was going to climb the cliff, we both have our own ways of chilling when we're not sailing and he opts for the Bear Grylls' agenda, while I favour placid staring.

When the world is completely silent in the early morning, I become entranced by the blue expanse stretching in front of me. Some people would say I just veg out, but actually I imagine all the waters joining up around the world, part of a giant unfettered stream circling the earth that all the wanderers throughout the ages have travelled along. Through this, in some way, the small adventurers like me and Seb are linked through time, space and this huge body of water, with all the others who have felt an irresistible urge to go and find new things for themselves. And, OK, often I just veg out.

I had been happily indulging in a strong bout of placid staring for about half an hour, when I noticed that both PLBs were lying next to me. I began to look around the lower half of the cliff for Seb. I couldn't see him.

I'm aware that my vision isn't perfect, but there appeared to be a completely empty vertical cliff in front of me. As well as the PLBs, I now noticed that all the water and all the meagre amount of food we had left, was piled at my feet. I began to feel slightly uneasy.

I went to the base of the cliff to inspect it more closely. Finding the end of the path, I started up it. After a few steps I hesitated; I knew Seb. This was a safe, slow, sane route to the top. He wouldn't have taken it.

By now I was well worked up. I was enveloped by an eerie fateful feeling, and the peace I had relished during my spate of placid staring, seemed to change into the oppressive stillness of a morgue.

I shouted, and my voice came back at me, pressing down as if to emphasise that there was no longer anyone there to hear it.

For almost an hour I stalked the cliff base, craning my head to see any sign of Seb. My throat was constricted by a massive lump. What should I do? Should I climb and try to find him?

I discovered his flip-flops, but the way up from their location looked frankly, impossible, and there was no sign of anything Seb-like that I could see from there. As I circled once again in my treadmill march from end to end of the cliff, I saw a piece of mud detach itself from the face and begin reeling over the sand.

I began to run. The tall piece of mud became clearer. It was scratched all up its legs and all over its chest and arms.

"Seb! Christ Seb! Are you all right?"

"Don't talk to me, I'm going in the water."

I watched him float, spread-eagled on the surface. After a while he rubbed his hands through his hair and a muddy cloud ballooned around his head. I lay out the food and water, which he consumed silently sitting on our towel.

"That's the most frightening thing I've done in my life."

I nodded. We sat.

When we were ready, we pulled Rocky into the water and got the sails up.

"OK if I have a siesta?" Seb asked

"Fine"

We wanted to get to Cala San Vicente today as Joe and Mo from MOJOs Marine Help had said it was the best place for us to start our longest leg from, and they'd promised to deliver food to us there. We only had five biscuits left and a long sail in front of us.

Seb's siesta seemed to do him good and we were sailing well with the wind on a broad reach. I was helming and then, suddenly, there was a fin.

"Oh my god, Seb! Dolphins!"

By the time he turned round the fin had continued in its downward arc. I held my breath, we'd waited so long for this moment. I was terrified the fin wouldn't come back up and Seb would think I was kidding him.

"Oh, wow!" Seb breathed as three fins broke the surface.

They weren't wonderfully close and there were only three of them, but they were undoubtedly dolphins and just seeing them was magical. I don't know if everyone gets the same reaction to seeing wild dolphins, but for me there's an overwhelming feeling of gratitude, of being allowed to witness something so perfect, so properly free, so joyful. Neither Seb nor I could stop smiling. It was the undisputed highlight of our trip so far, and we duly noted everything about them on our megafauna sheet.

Seb: As we sailed across Pollença Bay we were feeling great. We were more than half way through our journey and we had finally seen dolphins.

"Shall I try to call up Joe?" I asked Nick who was happy on the helm.

"Go for it."

The phone didn't ring more than twice before I heard Joe's friendly voice.

"MOJOS Marine Help …"

"Hi Joe, it's Sebastian in Rocky ..."

"Seb! Great to hear from you, what do you need?"

Nick couldn't stop himself from chorusing with me, "FOOD!"

"OK, are you heading for Cala San Vicente? We'll be over later."

"Awesome!" Nick said as I put the phone back inside it's two dry bags. "What very, very, very nice people!"

We weren't heeling, so I was sitting opposite Nick to balance the boat. Whatever it was, it was over in a moment, but Nick's gaze froze by my right shoulder as an involuntary yell left his parted lips.

I turned, but was only in time to see row upon row of ripples emanating from a deep circle about thirty metres away.

"What was it?"

"A thing ... a huge sea creature ... it just erupted, right there. My god! Where the hell is it now?" He started glancing nervously over the sides and for a moment I thought he was losing it.

"Maybe we should call up Brad and tell him it was a huge fish being chased by a Great White," I said in an attempt to get Nick to lighten up. "He'd arrive in a nanosecond and then we'd get to see his daughter." We'd been feeling a bit sore that baby Naia had not yet put in an appearance.

Nick was still looking concerned, and I tried to appear more serious to match his intensity. I only needed to think about how long we had waited to see dolphins.

The fact that we'd got to Day Seven before seeing any at all awakened a sense of urgency in me about how much our sea creatures need protection from us. When I'm close to dolphins I'm filled with a sense of deep respect, I feel humbled by them, yet I know human fishing methods and pollution are costing the lives of thousands of these magnificent beings.

"We can't tell Brad it was a Great White," Nick piped up, back to normal once again. "That would be a lie. I'm certain it was the Loch Ness Monster."

When we posted this on our blog later that evening, there were comments that we had been at the medicinal rum, so Nick wants me to make it clear that he was alcohol free. However, he will admit he can't be sure what it was as he didn't have time to see an entity or a body, it was just a massive splash, like a bomb going off. In a spooky aftermath, a month later a large tuna was found off Pollença with an enormous bit out of it. From the size and shape of the wound, local boffins decided it had been made by a four and a half metre long Great White Shark. Needless to say, Brad instantly set out in a boat to look for it, but the weather closed in and he had no luck. To us, this sounded even more frightening than Nessie, and we were in the right area ...

It was to be our day of adrenaline surges and our next one came as we were rounding the point to head down to Cala San Vicente. Evening was coming on and the wind was dropping, we were no longer able to move at any useful speed.

"Do we have right of way?"

"Course!"

"He'll have to turn ... he will turn... won't he?"

A commercial trawler was closing on us incredibly fast. Great waves were coming off its bow as the arms of its nets stuck out from either side. We couldn't see anyone on the bridge or on the part of the deck visible to us.

"MOVE!!!"

We crashed the boom across and literally slid under his stern. A bunch of fishermen suddenly looked up from their work. They at least had the courtesy to appear shocked, but we were too busy trying to jibe into their wake to even swear at them. Neptune must have been looking out for us as we just managed to get the bow round as the first wave hit. It swamped us completely and everything in Rocky was soaking, but if we hadn't turned and had taken it on the side, there's no doubt it would have rolled us over in a heartbeat.

We were more than relieved when the little beach at Cala San Vicente hove into view. Almost before we touched the sand we were met by the life guard who told us we could not stop there and that we needed to go around to the larger beach. Tired and hungry we complied only because we felt we had to. As it turned out, if we had not carried on to the second beach we would have missed one of the most incredible evenings of our life.

At the larger beach there were still loads of families covering the sand, but we had no hesitation about heading straight in. Joe was coming with food, this was no time to mess about.

As the sand crunched underneath Rocky's bow we were forced to have a quick rethink. Two burly pedalo guys were approaching and we thought we were going to be asked to leave again. They were big, they were fit and this time there were two of them.

"This isn't a good place," one of them began, as my heart sank down to my wet feet. "If the Guardia Civil come down you'll get a fine straight away."

Patiently we explained we had to stop here, this was the only viable place to start from if we were to make Sa Calobra tomorrow.

"It's your gamble," the smaller one replied.

"We'll give you a hand carrying it up to the top of the beach, it'll be safer there," the other chimed in as smiles ran all around our faces. What great guys!

With four of us, we picked up Rocky like she was a bath tub toy.

"This is fantastic," Nick said, to our friendly giants, "but how will we get her back in the water?"

"No problema!" they informed us. They started work at 9am and would give us a hand.

We'd only just finished thanking them when Joe, Mo and Sebastian turned up.

Never, in the whole of human history has fresh hot chicken tasted so magnificent. This was not a normal chicken, it was a chicken god, a chicken of greater succulence than any previous chicken, every bit of it was created to be savoured and have appreciative slurping noises made over it, we were in chicken heaven.

If you've never been really hungry, with a mouth like the Sahara, you may think I'm exaggerating. I'm not. That cold drink and chicken were the best things that have ever gone down my throat and I'm sure I'll have dreams about them for the rest of my life.

Joe had also brought us bread, water and tins for our dry bag, plus a VHF radio with which we could call up the Soller marina boss, Jaime Gonzalo, who had offered us a berth, food and shower.

We were still chatting to Joe and Mo through happy mouthfuls when some children came over and began asking questions about Rocky. An elegant blonde lady with piercing eyes wandered over to see what was interesting her young charges.

"Oh my goodness, you're the SailAid boys," she said clapping her hands to her mouth. "My friend told me on Facebook this morning to look out for you in Pollença, and I totally forgot and came here with the children instead! You must come home with us for the night."

Nick is standing next to Dina. We were amazed that, with so many nieces to look after, she had taken two grubby teens under her wing too. We had an incredible evening before setting off on the longest leg of our voyage.

Today had been major, and now a complete stranger was insisting we accept lashings of hospitality.

"Really? Are you sure?" we said weakly.
"Of course. Maybe you should phone your parents and tell them you're going home with Dina Rosenmeier.

"They can Google me by typing in "A Journey in my mother's footsteps", then they'll know you are going to be OK."

Nick: I was trying to pack up the things we needed to take to Dina's house but my phone was going bonkers with texts. It appeared Mum had Googled Dina.

"OMG babe! She's a film director. Made the film A Journey in My Mother's Footsteps and received great reviews. It's about her Mum who worked with street orphans in India during the 1970s."

The phone beeped again: "She's an actress too. Danish. Loads about her. Couldn't have happened on a better night. Off to party now, love u."

The party was for Seb's sister. It was Big Alice's 19th birthday. Mum had offered to pick us up and take us to the party as a surprise, but we didn't feel comfortable about being so far away from Rocky and, as it turned out, we'd been temporarily adopted by a film star. I love Alice and all that stuff, but chances like this don't come along too often and I was going to make the most of it.

We were soon packed into Dina's stylish convertible. I was in the front beside our hostess and Seb was in the back sandwiched between some of her nieces. Apart from the littlest one, they all spoke amazingly good English and we were instantly engulfed back into a noisy happy family. I felt immediately at home.

Dina was explaining the quirks of the shower that we would be using.

"It has three knobs which can be a little confusing. They're for the jets, temperature and pressure."

It sounded simple enough to me and I melted into the comfy car seat, letting her words wash over me and enjoying the squeals from the back and the continual banter. On one level everything felt wonderfully familiar, but then the conversation would be peppered with sentences like, "When I was working with Angelina Jolie ..." and "I prefer Europe to Hollywood, when I lived there ..." which made me pinch myself to check I wasn't dreaming on my li-lo.

When we arrived at Dina's house, Seb was ushered into the enormous bathroom first. He claimed not to have been able to hear anything in the back seat, so I gave him a quick run through and left him to it.

Back upstairs, I was having a great time playing with the nieces. We'd told Dina about Big Alice's birthday and she suggested we Skype the party so we could feel part of it, which was brilliant.

About fifteen minutes later Seb appeared wrapped in a towel, looking hunted. He approached me in a furtive kind of way, almost brushing off a handful of nieces in his urgency to get next to my ear.

"Quick, run down and turn that thing off! I've tried EVERYTHING! The bloody thing's possessed!"

"I told you, the bottom knob controls the ..."

"Just do it!" he hissed.

This was clearly a desperate man. I left expecting to discover a scene reminiscent of the Sorcerer's Apprentice.

Once I too was washed and we'd all sung Happy Birthday to Big Alice and swallowed down the lumps that swelled in our throats when we heard all our families celebrating together – the Skype wouldn't work as they were sitting on the beach in Peguera - Dina suggested we went out to enjoy the town fiestas that were taking place in Pollença that weekend.

We had a fantastic evening in the town's main square, dancing, eating and being absorbed into this amazing family. They didn't hold back at all. The kids were totally mental, even Little Alice – who isn't known for being conventional – could have learnt something from them!

On the way back to Dina's we stopped opposite a house where the complete ground floor was full of a collection of pristine classic cars. The automobiles (the word "car" was far too normal for them) were surrounded by acres of plate glass so that everyone could ogle this sumptuous exhibition, which was seriously generous of the owner.

It had been a roller-coaster day and as I dropped into bed I felt choked by deep gratitude to Dina and her family, and to whatever had kept us alive during our encounter with the fishing boat, and Seb's cliff climbing escapade, also to Jo, Mo and Sebastian for the most memorable chicken ever, and to the marvelous dolphins for finally showing themselves. What a day!

Day Eight

Nick: I awoke to aromas that made my mouth water so much I was out of bed in a flash. Dina was cooking us an enormous breakfast, and she had even washed our shirts and swimmers, which had been completely humming.

Today we would be tackling out longest and most difficult leg of the journey. Between Cala San Vicente and Sa Calobra there is nowhere to run for shelter if things go wrong. The entire stretch consists of towering rock cliffs which cause fluky winds and a micro climate that is frequently completely different to the rest of the island. This was the part Captain Kevin had warned us about when he told us to keep the sheets in our hands and never cleat off anything.

By 9 o'clock we were back at Rocky, armed with sandwiches and Pringles for the journey. There was absolutely no wind and it was beginning to rain. This was a worry; we had a long way to go. At 11 o'clock we decided to paddle out and see if we could find a breeze. We put up full sail in the hope that it would catch any breath of action we were lucky enough to encounter.

A large black fin appeared some way off the port bow and I prepared myself for a megafauna display, but the animal was making far more speed than we were and we saw no more of it. If we weren't travelling at a reasonable rate by noon we would have to think about returning to the beach and trying another day. Rocky has no lights, so arriving at Sa Calobra after dark wasn't an option.

We were still reeling from the hospitality we had received from Dina, it had been hard to say goodbye to her and the nieces. Although we'd only been with them for a few hours, they felt like old friends.

"It was amazing," Seb reminisced while idly wiggling the tiller in the hope that it might lead to forward motion, "apart from that shower ... that was horrible!"

"I loved it."

"Why three knobs?!"

"Do I have to explain this to you again?"

"You'll only explain it wrong again!"

"As I've said before, apparently unsuccessfully, it was very simple, the bottom knob controlled whether the water was going to come out of the side jets, the shower or the bath taps, although I'll admit you had to jiggle it a bit. The middle knob, if you turned it anti-clockwise got increasingly hot but the pressure stayed the same, and it technically also controlled the on and off. While the top one controlled what part of the shower the water came out of ... the hose or the top. The jets were part of the bath knob at the bottom, or something like that ..."

Seb remained unconvinced in spite of my painstakingly clear description.

"It was a struggle from the start. Water came out of everywhere. I couldn't get the temperature right and the pressure kept changing. I was turning taps the entire time in every direction and getting alternately scalded and frozen by jets attacking me all over my body completely at random. I had no option but to escape from its clutches. I'd spent three quarters of the time I was in there trying to turn it off, and failing miserably."

"Took me a second."

"Luck, pure luck. That thing was evil!"

Seb: There was hardly time to register the approach of ripples on the water before the wind hit us and the jib snapped full with such force I thought it would blow out. In an instant we went from zero wind to more than we had ever sailed in before. We hadn't reefed.

I was fighting to hang onto the tiller as Rocky lurched onto her side dragging gallons of water into the cockpit. Nick was clambering up a near vertical surface, leaning as far out as he could, to try and balance the pull of our ridiculously large sail area.

From believing I was now good at handling Rocky, I realised immediately that I was no longer in control. The most I could do was react as quickly as possible to whatever the next gale force gust did to us.

We progressed via a series of half capsizes, dropping the sheets whenever Rocky's angle threatened to throw us into the sea, so her bow slewed round off the wave it was riding and the water would then hit us from the opposite side, threatening to swamp the boat whichever way we turned.

Tentatively Nick would haul in the sheets again and I would turn Rocky's nose so she would bite back into the maelstrom. Although the waves were pushing us away from the deadly unyielding walls, they were on our side and continually soaked us.

Teeth chattering, as fresh deluges of cold water crashed over us every few seconds, salty wet ropes of hair whipped around my eyes making it almost impossible to see, yet, at times in my peripheral vision, there seemed to be a presence. Something white and sturdy, that wasn't doing an impression of a bucking bronco, was on our seaward side.

In the brief moment while we wallowed in the

aftermath of another near capsize, I saw her properly. It was a white catamaran with four or five people on deck. Unlike us, they had shortened sail and were taking wide controlled tacks. Rocky's jib snapped full again and we were back surfing parallel to the gigantic cliffs at eight or nine knots. Neither of us had time to do anything other than fight to remain upright and inside the boat. But now I knew there was someone watching us, someone who could help if I really couldn't hang onto this tiller any longer.

My arms felt as if they were being dragged out of my shoulders, and my calves were beginning to cramp and tremble from the constant strain between the foot straps and my bizarre body angle. Nick flicked cascades of water from his hair, his hands showing angry red welts where the sheets were sawing their way into his unprotected flesh. In our clothes bag there were two pairs of sailing mittens. When we left this morning we had been worried we would have to turn back because of millpond conditions. Now we had no way of turning anywhere much, or reefing, or getting anything out of the bags, we just had to carry on until it stopped, or the worst happened.

Nick: At Punta Beca we suddenly lost the wind, completely. Skidding to a halt in the space of a few boat lengths, I was finally able to look across at our guardian angel. She was turning in a smooth half circle, her gallant white hulls gliding off, their protective vigil abruptly over.

I don't know who the crew of that catamaran were, but I would like to thank them. We had never sailed like that before in our lives and you knew we were in trouble but had the patience to let us see if we could handle it, and the kindness to shadow us in case we couldn't. Just having you there made a bad situation far less terrifying. If I ever meet you, and I'm old enough to buy beer, I owe you a barrel!

Once we'd slowly and painfully uncurled our hands from tiller and sheets, and then indulged in a bit of nervous laughter, we turned our attention to trying to find the Pringles and sandwiches.

Seb was digging about in the bags with one hand on the flaccid jib sheet while I was nudging the tiller with my knee and untangling the main sheet from its heap on the floor. A blast of air hit us like two express trains passing, and Rocky groaned as the sails bent her away from the latest onslaught. We were flying again but this time the waves were rolling into us hard on the aft quarter. There was no room for error given our tiny amount of freeboard. It felt as if the sea had tested Seb's helming skills and now it had to do the same to me. The jib was snatching like crazy and there were several notable moments when I was canning it. The force of the wind in the sails and the weight of the waves crashing over us from the side seemed certain to crush us. We were cold, soaking and every body cell seemed to be wearing a sapping crust of salt.

On and on the solid walls went, marching down the side of Mallorca, blocking the way to any safety from the fury of the summer wind.

A part of me began to panic that we had missed the entrance and would have to continue many miles further until we reached Soller. The day had turned into an endless battle and we would not dare to jinx our chances by guessing which side would win.

Many times a shadow on the cliff tricked my brain

into premature relief, thinking I was seeing the start of the only inlet on this part of the coast; the only possible respite from our endless helter-skelter ride.

When the narrow entrance came into view it was like looking at a cosy lounge with comfy chairs, a crackling fire and an oblivious family playing Scrabble, when you're outside the window in a hurricane. We surfed headlong for the thin opening and as the rocks overshadowed us we flowed into a breathtakingly beautiful haven where wonder replaced havoc.

Our tiny tent pitched on the beach at the Torrent de Pareis.

Seb: "I've found the Pringles," I called out to Nick as we unloaded everything from Rocky in an attempt to dry off a bit.

It was Saturday so the main beach, which is backed by the Torrent de Pareis, was too crowded for us to approach. Instead we had turned right into the small port and pulled up on a narrow stretch of shingle. It wasn't ideal, but we needed food and water before we thought of Plan B.

A woman was nursing her baby on a terrace that backed onto where we were. She asked us what we were doing and offered to let us eat on her terrace so we could sit at a table. She clearly knew the coastline exceedingly well because she gave us loads of information about tiny bays we hadn't even considered going into.

Nick phoned his Mum to say we'd arrived. "That's amazing," she replied when he told her we'd made it to Sa Calobra, "there's been no wind here all day so I packed a strobe light to guide you in. I thought you'd be rowing."

"Mum, believe me, we were the furthest away from rowing you can imagine!" I heard him say.

The Mums decided to drive up together bearing food, clean T-shirts and contact lenses, so once we'd emptied Rocky we lay back and relaxed. I would never have believed shingle could feel so luxurious. We hadn't seen any further sign of Nessie or the dolphins today, but to be honest we could have been attacked by a giant squid and failed to notice as we were seriously preoccupied with survival at the time.

When they arrived the Mums gave us a minor tongue-lashing for not putting in a reef before leaving Cala San Vicente, but before they could get into full flow, the lady with the baby called out.

"Estefania?"

Our latest very nice person turned out to have been a work colleague of Steph's at the local sail training organisation, Joves Navegants, from years back. So, by weird coincidence the two of them had lots of catching up to do and we discovered exactly why our lady, Barbara, knew the island's coastline as well as she did.

Once most of the tourists had left the beach we decided to row Rocky round to the Torrent de Pareis. The scenery is so majestic it feeds your soul and we didn't want to miss this chance to soak it up.

What we didn't realise before we'd paddled and

pitched our tent, was that the two fresh water pools behind the beach ensure that while your soul is being fed, your body is providing a gourmet meal for swarms of mosquitoes.

To add to the other-worldliness of this place were four swans. They drifted on the pools backed by towering mountains as the sun began dropping and a blaze of fire lit the entrance.

Watching the four swans on the fresh water pools that backed the beach at Mallorca's spectacular Torrent de Pareis.

Day Nine

Seb: We had tried to get rid of all the mozzies from inside the tent before we zipped it closed, but some had hidden, and by dawn they were obese.

It was Sunday morning and the complete tranquillity of our surroundings was destined to be filled with towels and sun umbrellas within an hour. As we breakfasted we knew we were seeing Sa Calobra at its very best. We wanted to leave before things got noisy and the magic was rubbed out by normality, so we started paddling even though there was no wind, and the few zephyrs we found were against us.

Although we had a tempting offer of food and a shower from the boss of Soller marina, we hoped to by-pass it and get as far as Port Valldemossa. This was a pity because Soller is beautiful. Pete and Steph got engaged there in 1988, and we could have really enjoyed an evening wandering along the front and listening to the gentle hoot of the tram. However, we were aware we were beginning to get tired, it was time to make a final few days' effort and run for home.

By the time we drew level with Cala Tuent we had a slight breeze and I could feel a siesta coming on, so I handed the tiller to Nick.

Half an hour later, feeling refreshed, I cracked open my eyes to a most unpleasant sight.

"What the hell have you been doing?"

"Oh, hi Dude, you're awake."

"Nick! You've gone backwards! When I went to sleep we were level with the entrance, and now we're just behind it!"

"No wind, mate."

This was bad. At this rate we wouldn't even make

Soller. The first wave of despondency swept over me. It's monotonous and frustrating to be marooned in the sun for hours and achieve no headway at all. Although we knew it would make us hot and thirsty and not accomplish much, we decided to paddle. It was better than doing nothing. Exceedingly slowly, we drew level with the entrance again, and, as we did, it seemed as if we crossed an invisible line where the wind began to blow.

Finally we were smiling again, there was wind on the water, and just in front of us there was a big circle that looked slightly different. At the same time as I noticed the circle, a pod of about twenty dolphins broke the surface, leaping out of the water and then dashing around one another. They were playing so happily right in front of us and this time we had some wind and could follow them.

"I want to video them," I said, grabbing the camera we had permanently tied to the base of the mast.

Nick's face was a study in bliss and I reckoned I must look the same to him. The dolphins were jumping in pairs and trios; they were the world's best synchronised swimmers. We could see their smiling faces, the power of their movements through the water, the lazy kindness of their eyes.

Nick was doing his best to sail as close to them as he could although he must have been torn between watching the display and concentrating on the sails.

After about fifteen minutes the circle of action separated into two and one half of the dolphins moved further out to sea while the others turned towards the far point of land, we could still see them so we kept sailing with the closer group, but they were, by now, too far away to film. When they eventually outstripped our eyes we sat back in Rocky, overflowing with the warmest fuzziest feeling you can possibly imagine.

"Let's have a look at the video," Nick said, handing me the tiller and fiddling with the rewind button.

I thought his silence was because he was struggling to put into words the awesomeness of my recording. I waited patiently to give him time to construct the sentence that contained the phrase "... next David Attenborough..."

"Pitiful!"

I grabbed the camera off him and viewed five full minutes of the lens periodically leaping upwards and achieving a stunning film of the sky without a single sea mammal in sight. I was gutted.

"They kept jumping and I didn't want to miss them so I had to keep looking up."

"Lame Dude! Really lame."

The fuzziness might have worn off a little, but I was determined to get them next time.

By now we had a good wind behind us and were confident of passing Soller although it was debatable whether we'd be pulling into Deya or Valldemossa. Deya's beach is completely stony so we'd been hoping to avoid it as we knew hauling Rocky out would be a problem.

"Nick! Look! Fin!"

It was only ten metres away from us and coming straight towards the boat.

Although the fin was triangular, I didn't really think it was a shark because it appeared a bit floppy, but whatever it was, it was certainly big, and aiming for us.

The fin sank beneath the surface and I began scanning the ripples to try and see where it had gone.

Nick: "Seb!?!"

A massive shadow was forming right next to the boat behind Seb's shoulder. It was round and covered about three-quarters of Rocky's length. I admit it, I was seriously close to defecation, any fish aggression at this point and I would have lost it.

Just as Seb looked round and clocked what was behind him the shadow suddenly took off and then the fin reappeared fifteen metres behind us.

"I think that was a Pez Luna," Seb said once we'd calmed down and were recording the event on our megafauna sheet. "They can grow up to five metres wide, so that was a smallish one."

"Big enough!" I said, attempting to keep my voice deep and manly, although probably failing totally.

By now we had passed Deya and were confident of making Valldemossa.

"Maybe we should pull in there," I said pointing to a small beach. It looked really nice and since our conversation with Barbara I'd become eager to explore some of the bays that weren't named on the chart.

"It's got a road going down, so it should be OK," Seb agreed.

Mum loves this part of the island and had said she'd drive over with dinner if we were accessible. We could see Port Valldemossa not far off but at the weekend we reckoned it was likely to be crowded until late, while on this beach we could only see a couple of people.

We began sailing in. By now we had "beach

approach" down to a fine art. It was always someone's turn to jump out. The "jumper" would be steering while the other one would feel the depth with a paddle and control the centre-plate. As soon as the "feeler" touched the bottom easily, the "jumper" would leap in – usually up to their knees.

"Off you go," Seb said confidently as I saw his paddle not go more than half-way down.

I put my feet over the side expecting to touch ground; I wriggled a bit further, and still found nothing solid. By now I was hanging off Rocky, pulling her further and further over, so I thought I'd better let go. I descended up to my neck.

Hauling my head back up Rocky's side again, with the intention of telling Seb his sounding technique was useless, I found a completely empty boat. The *Marie Celeste* had been re-enacted just next to Valldemossa. What the hell was going on?

I dropped down to think about it, then hauled myself up for another look.

The cockpit was still empty but from the corner of my eye I saw a head. Seb was swimming towards me.

"What did you leave the boat for?" I yelled across at him. "I thought we had a system for this!" Honestly, sometimes he could do the weirdest things!

"Leave the boat?" He managed to shout and splutter at the same time. "Like I had a choice when a total moron decided to catapult me through the air at terminal velocity! Whatcha do that for?"

"You told me to jump!"

"Yes, exactly, so why did you decide to take Rocky with you and then suddenly let go?"

After a bit of swimming we discovered Seb had managed to "sound" the only rock in the bay with his paddle, so we settled on fifty/fifty blame.

The two guys on the beach were watching us. Now that we were closer we could see that the "bay" was no more than a couple of metres of sand and a boat house. I was half expecting them to tell us to go away, but as we staggered through the shallows, pulling Rocky behind us, they grabbed a side each and helped us lift her as far as it was possible to go.

Xisco and Jose Miguel owned the boat house. Within minutes they had produced four ice-cold beers from a cool box. We sat and chatted. They were very, very nice people, and their beer was very, very nice too. They offered us a shower from their hose pipe, so we were able to enjoy a wonderful swim – where we luckily dodged all the jellyfish – before getting clean. It was fantastic to get rid of the salt. We'd been crusty since the first splash out of Cala San Vicente, and there had been a lot of splashes and half drownings since then. Fresh water and a "cool tube", as my Australian cousins would put it, made me feel human again.

As the beach was very rocky and narrow, Xisco advised us to pitch the tent on the roof of the boathouse which was a flat piece of cement quite a bit further up the cliff. Even though we'd brought Rocky up the beach we tied her painter to a pole and then went back up to make camp.

Xisco and Jose Miguel said a final "adiós" and left us a full melon before driving off up the mountain side. We sat and gorged ourselves on our juicy first course. Seb had sent Mum a Google dot, so all she had to do was follow it and main course plus desert would arrive shortly. We felt like we were on the final night of "I'm a Celebrity, Get Me Out of Here" where they get fed a slap up meal after days of eating cockroaches … not that we'd had to eat bugs, but you know what I mean.

"She's taking a while," I said to Seb a little later. Sailing all day makes us ridiculously tired and by eight o'clock we're dying to clean our teeth and turn in. It was 7.30.

Seb's phone rang.

"I'm trying to find you, but your dot ends on a cliff. Are you close enough to walk to Port Valldemossa?"

We explained that, as walking on water wasn't one of our specialities, that would be tricky, but that Xisco and Jose Miguel left by car, so there must be a simple route down to us.

Half an hour later she phoned again.

"I'm at the restaurant directly above your dot, they say that all the roads around you are private and many are barred, they've shown me where to turn so if there's no gate you'll get dinner in about fifteen minutes."

Result!

"What are you bringing?" I couldn't help myself, I needed to know ... to have time with my imagination. I was hungry!

"Hot sausage pasta and banoffi muffins plus some bits for tomorrow."

My saliva became disgustingly overactive.

Twenty minutes later she called again.

"Sorry guys, there was a massive gate with a padlock. I hope you've got some tins left."

"Mum! You can't do this! I'm already tasting it! You should never have told us!"

But she had gone, with a car-full of still warm banoffi muffins that had been so tantalisingly close I fancied I could smell them. By now it was deep dusk, time for tin opening rather than running around on a cliff face trying to find a source of sausage pasta.

As we sat on our roof we were treated to the most fantastic sunset. When it burned itself out, we lay down in our tent and drifted into sleep, lulled by the song of the surf below us. I wouldn't have missed it for the world.

Looking down from our camping platform on the boat house roof, we could see Rocky as we were treated to a wonderful sunset.

Day Ten

Nick: Although there was no wind, we started paddling at 8.30 and afterwards we discovered that someone had taken photos of us still paddling at 9.34 and posted them on Facebook.

Eventually we got a little wind from behind and ghosted along at a couple of knots. We'd had a problem with the tiller extension for a few days. The screw head had broken and it had come loose so we tied it against the tiller with a piece of elastic in the hope that if we stopped using it regularly, when we were trying to avoid capsize and really needed it, we'd still have it. Somehow the elastic came undone. It was one of those things that happen before you've really registered what's going on. The tiller extension dropped neatly over the side and sank incredibly fast. Seb was very annoyed because he was on the tiller at the time, but to be honest, it could have happened to either of us. We'll have to moderate our sailing from now on, if possible.

We were beginning to get bored of idling along when Seb breathed, "Oh my god! Dolphins!"

I jumped up.

"Just over there," he said pointing directly off the port bow.

I was looking twenty or thirty metres away when they leapt, no more than five metres from Rocky, in a perfect synchronised arch; the soft "puuuff" from their blow holes sounded together, their long, grey muscular bodies flexed just in front of me. It was the most magnificent sight of my life.

"There!!!!!" I screamed at the top of my voice, leaping to my feet, and then, immediately, I realised what I had done.

I had been so surprised, I hadn't expected them to be so close.

This was the lowest point of the trip for me. Directly that one word was out of my mouth, my heart seemed to buckle in on itself. "You bloody idiot!" I thought, "you complete and utter dickhead". I was so upset and I knew that Seb was too.

"What the hell did you do that for?" he growled through a corner of his mouth.

The next time the dolphins surfaced they were forty metres off and moving away fast.

"Don't try to make me feel better," I mumbled

"Wasn't planning on it," came Seb's curt reply.

I sat hunched over my jib sheet and proceeded to hate myself.

In the narrow channel between Dragonera and Mallorca we had our second near-death experience with a fishing boat. There seems to be a general acceptance that it's OK to push the throttle down and leave the autopilot on with nobody on watch, but it was impossible for us to see that there was no-one in the wheelhouse, until it was almost too late.

"Dude? They are going to give way, aren't they?"

"Got to ... haven't they?"

"J I B E !!!!"

The channel was so narrow that we could only turn straight into their wake and were promptly swamped by it. Rocky wallowed full of water while the fishing boat sped on completely oblivious.

Half an hour later, it happened again.

This time we didn't wait as long to get out of the way.

We'd realised, there's never anyone on watch. But this trawler was going even faster than the previous one, creating even bigger waves that were really dangerous.

We fought to stop the cresting wake from hitting our side. It would have annihilated us. The space between trough and breaking top is so close together in a big wake that a boat Rocky's size doesn't have time to climb out of the trough before the crest rolls you over and breaks on top of you.

I was really mad now, these guys didn't give a shit.

"Why the hell don't those bastards slow down! What percentage of power boats out here have had the decency to think "let's slow down and not swamp those lads"?"

"About one per cent," Seb replied, "on a good day."

Seb: But it wasn't a good day, even though we did cover a good distance.

We decided to make landfall in Cala Cranc. We were still shaken by the double encounter with unmanned fishing boats, but now we were in an inshore yachting area so we didn't expect a re-run.

As we were heading into the cala a massive American-flagged superyacht steamed past us at ridiculous speed. The wake it created was so high I got that roller-coaster tummy feeling, of leaving your stomach at the top while the rest of you crashes down. There were three waves and the third completely soaked everything. If there had been a fourth it would have wiped us out; and if any of them had hit us on the side it would have been "bye-bye", capsize, sunk. The whole area was unexpectedly scary because of the number of fast moving pleasure boats. They came from all directions and, as we still didn't know who had right of way, and didn't trust any of the motor boats to know either, we kept having to tack and jibe into their wake just to ensure we didn't get run down.

We had just got into clearer water and back on an even keel when a llaut called "Dragonera" chugged past us. The people aboard seemed to be staring. Then they turned round and came straight towards us.

"Ahoy there Rocky!" a lady shouted. "We love your blog! We've followed you all the way round."

We were grinning like imbeciles, all thoughts of murderous superyachts immediately swept from our minds. This was wicked!

"We've only got this bar of chocolate and a bottle of water I'm afraid, but it's cold and we'd love you to have it. Well done guys!"

And the very, very nice people were handing us vittles at just the time we had absolutely no food left at all. Someone was looking after us, that was certain, especially in the light of what happened later in the evening.

Cala Cranc doesn't have an ideal beach. A steep shale slope is backed by a tiny platform, and that's it, but we pulled Rocky up as high as we could and settled down to do justice to the chocolate before it melted. At that time our only companions were goats, so we hoped someone would come down later and we could ask them to give us a hand hauling Rocky further up the incline.

We phoned in our position and as Cala Cranc is only about fifteen minutes' drive from my house, Mum said she'd come down and watch the sun set with us … armed with a pizza. I was so happy!

Nick had told his mum about the dolphin-shouting disaster and looked disgusted when he got off the phone.

"Apparently dolphins like it if you whistle at them," he said. "Why the hell do parents spend all your childhood telling you useless things like how to tidy your room, and totally omit vital pieces of information like the fact that you should whistle at dolphins! Incredible!"

He was about to sit down and have a really good mope when I mentioned the pizza.

"Awesome! Have you sent her our exact position?"

"Of course."

He thought for a while.

"We can't leave this to chance you know, not after last night. I'm going to the top to find a road name."

"It's only a few minutes' drive, there's no need."

"Dude! Get serious! This is pizza!"

He disappeared off the beach, camera in hand to film the mountain goats that we were now sharing our camp space with, focused upon a mission to find the name of the closest place to park. If he'd had a balloon or two he would definitely have blown them up and attached them along the route so that Mum could home in on us more easily. He was dreaming about that pizza.

I was just enjoying a few Z-eds when I became conscious that a camera was pointing at me. Opening an eye, I was jerked awake by Nick's grinning face in front of me. He was still hopping about in a worried frenzy of pizza anticipation.

"I hope your Google dot works because when I

got to the top I found all the roads had been dug up and there were no road signs of any description. I asked a few people what the road was called, but nobody seemed to know, it's all new."

"Chill Nick. It will be fine," at times I could get the urge to swot Nick, especially if I was in mid-doze and he was excited about something. "You could pitch the tent; she's bound to be here in a minute."

"OK" and he cantered off to get busy with li-los. Ten minutes later my phone rang.

"I'm here. Where are you?"

"Well, I'm here. Where are you?"

"Seb-as-ti-an! I've got twenty per cent battery left on my phone so don't mess about."

We described what the area looked like and hoped that would do the trick. Half an hour later she rang again.

"I've had enough! I'm not doing this any longer …"

Mum seemed a little stressed. We were in danger of losing our pizza. It was a red alert situation.

"Mum, please, you must be practically on top of us …" we begged, we cajoled, we convinced her to keep trying.

"I'm going up to find her."

"OK, I'll get the sleeping bags in place and stuff," Nick said as I headed up the track.

Walking around at the top I prayed she'd turn down the road. She sounded seriously up tight. I didn't know which was scarier: Mum in her present state, or Nick if I returned pizza-less. As the darkness deepened I had no option but to return empty handed.

Luckily Nick was already asleep – although later he claimed he was just "resting his eyes" but couldn't see the point in opening them when there was no smell of melted cheese and oregano.

Suddenly, with a crack of branches, Mum literally slid down the bank into our camp, Tarzan style.

"I went down every road on this side of the island to find you," she said breathlessly as she placed the king-sized gungy prize in front of us. "That was a bloody nightmare! I've just scrambled down a cliff in the pitch black, fallen in goat's poo, got whipped round the face by branches ... that Bear Grylls, or whatever he's called, would never have done what I just did! It was like being in a Milk Tray advert, but with a pizza! I'm starving!"

This had been a massively troublesome pizza, but it may have been worth it because a miracle was about to occur right in front of my eyes.

Nick has one inviolable rule. Like Joey, out of the series Friends, he "doesn't share food". For Nick, food is a sacred thing, to be coveted like Smeagol with his ring, so to hear him say, "Have a piece of pizza" at any time would have been momentous, but when we were physically dying of hunger it was a total revelation!

After we'd all eaten and told Mum what had happened with the dolphins and the fishing boats, and she had got over missing the sunset and the fact that the goats poo was still stuck to her flip-flops, it was time to get her back.

"I'll walk you to the car," I said.

"Do you have a torch?"

"No."

It was the worst night we had experienced for heat. There wasn't a breath of wind and armies of mozzies were out in mega swarms, eager for blood. We tried everything to get comfortable, even opening the tent door to stick our feet outside, but so much of us was being consumed on a minute by minute basis, that we had to zip up again. Nick managed to nod off, but I was drenched in sweat. The sleeping bag beneath me was wet through. The air in the tent lay heavily on top of me, pushing down as if I were in a sauna. My arms stuck against my torso, my hair was plastered to my head, digesting the pizza seemed to have lit a furnace in my stomach. Although every part of my body was exhausted there was no possibility of me sleeping. For the past ten days neither of us had been awake after nine o'clock, tonight I saw my watch glow 23:30.

I heard a wave rush up the shale and raised my head to focus on the gauze window beside the door flap. I couldn't see anything. As a second wave hit the beach I fumbled for my glasses. Immediately I saw Rocky's mast swaying.

"Rocky's moving!" I said, almost as a matter of interest while gently shaking Nick and fumbling for the door zip. The moment I voiced it, a massive wave rumbled up the shore almost into the tent itself.

Nick erupted from his li-lo and elbowed me out of the way. He had closed the door and knew the exact position of the zip. We half flew out of the tent, stumbling onto the shale at the moment Rocky left the beach. Some giant hand had hold of her and was dragging her straight back towards the entrance of the bay and the wide open Mediterranean. She was travelling very, very fast.

Slippery rocks bordered the shoreline of the cala, and there was no light, or time, to see where they were. Nick literally dove head long over where he thought they ended. Rocky was vanishing into the blackness, our whole trip was being sucked out to sea, we had got so close to home and we were about to lose it all. I was crushed.

Every evening for ten days we had found someone to help us pull Rocky further up the beach. We had been ultra careful on the north west coast where we expected problems. Tonight we had been alone, it had been late and bruisingly humid. With just the two of us we'd strained every muscle to move the hull about an inch further up, before looking at each other and saying, "Yes, that's enough."

Looking back, I guess we were asking for it, but we were dog tired and we thought we'd get away with it.

Cala Cranc is wide open to the sea.

I felt physically sick thinking of all the money that had been pledged to Mediterranea, that they now wouldn't receive; of the number of people who would say "At least you tried", in an attempt to make me feel better, but would actually make me feel far, far worse than if they'd insulted me.

My throat was so choked by the enormity of what we'd lost that I was completely unable to answer when a husky voice came out of the blackness.

"Got her."

I was crawling up from the waterline, feeling for all the big rocks and rolling them out of the way. Together we pulled Rocky further than we'd ever dragged her before by ourselves, then we dug her anchor into the shale and put a rope around a rock at the back of the beach.

Shale is no good for anchors. We didn't feel confident she was safe yet.

There are two useless pulleys on Rocky's bow, plus a useless cleat that faces completely the wrong direction for anything to do with sailing. We have never discovered a purpose for any of them until that night. Between the pulleys and the rock, sweating buckets in the clammy heat, we jumped Rocky forward, centimetre by muscle-wrenching centimetre until she was on top of the beach's platform.

With deft professionalism Nick whipped an instant perfect bowline in the rock rope and the painter. She was on top of a hill with an anchor and two lines attaching her to the land. Finally we were satisfied.

We sat on the beach, totally pumped with adrenaline.

"We were soooo lucky," Nick said, almost to himself. "If you hadn't seen the mast go, we'd have been screwed."

"Imagine if we'd just woken up and Rocky was nowhere to be seen," I said, shuddering in the boiling night.

For the first time on our trip, we saw the stars. The sky was literally teeming with them. We lay back and watched them winking out of the night. Now that you actually looked up at them there seemed to be more light out there than dark. It was completely mesmerising.

"Well mate, at least we're certain you know how to tie a bowline now!"

Day Eleven

Seb: I woke up aching in muscles I hadn't even known existed before this morning. The sun was up but I felt more fatigued than at any time, day or night, during the entire trip. Pushing myself up onto my elbows required my last reserves of energy and I stopped there, trying to imagine myself at the end of today in Illetas with my friends.

It was a lovely image in itself; if only I could have slept in a comfy bed with a fan on me all day, I could then visualise myself being the life and soul of the party. But the reality was that we had to sail there first, and I was weak as a kitten.

Forcing myself out of the tent I saw Nick lying in the water floating on his back. I sat beside Rocky looking out at the empty bay, empty right to the horizon, with an empty blue sky above. Even in my knackered state I knew I was seriously lucky to live anywhere as beautiful as this.

Nick emerged from his oceanic bath tub and began rummaging in the food bag for breakfast. We had almost nothing left. A few suspect biscuits adorned with sand where the icing sugar should have been, a solitary tin of fruit salad and a tin of sardines. We ate in companiable silence. Nick was exceedingly quiet and I thought I caught him flinching a couple of times when he moved. I reckoned he was feeling as jaded as I was.

Someone by the name of Thomas Schepens Stevens had contacted our Facebook page and offered to restock our depleted food bag at his store in Santa Ponça. It was a very generous and tempting offer, but we quailed at the thought of sailing any further than we absolutely had to this morning. A detour into the deep bay of Santa Ponça, instead of holding our course straight across the entrance, wasn't going to happen in our enfeebled condition.

To a certain extent we'd got used to being hungry, and we knew our friends would bring a picnic to Illetas, we just had to get there.

Many people have asked how we managed normal bathroom activities on this trip, so it wouldn't be a full account if I left this important information out. Often we dug deep holes and then re-covered them, sometimes piling stones on top to deter any kids from digging in that part of the sand. On other days, if there was nobody around, we would swim out and "feed the fishes".

This morning there was no-one around. I swam far out, on the opposite side of the bay to Rocky, and left the fish a prodigious feast.

Not being a chef, I have no idea what they put in pizza, but I definitely now know it floats. Not only did it float, it stalked.

Having left it far away, close to the entrance, it pursued me, hunting against wind and current, moving indefatigably back towards Rocky. It arrived as we were preparing to leave.

"Dude! I'm not getting in the water with that!"

To be honest, nor was I. It may previously have been a part of me, but now it was on its own.

"If we throw stones at it, it will float away."

So we did. We strafed it with skimming stones, then pounded it with rocks before besieging it with boulders, but still the unbreakable poo bobbed behind Rocky.

We needed to re-arm. Building piles of ammunition along the shoreline, we showed cruelty without courage towards the former pizza we had craved so much.

Still it would not die.

Desperation rose in the ranks. Were we destined to be caged forever on Cala Cranc beach by the indestructible homing poo?

Almost weeping with exhausted frustration, Nick whispered, "Please, go away ... leave us ..." but the poo had no mercy.

Staying safely at the bow we began a final death-defying bid for freedom. We shoved Rocky's stern into the poo path and leapt aboard, wielding paddles at the poo to create a frenzied tidal wave that even this being of unusual fortitude was powerless to resist. It bobbed backwards, away from the port quarter. We had a mouse hole of opportunity before it swung to face us once more, but we were ready, and we took it. Yelping in triumph we pushed off with audacious determination and made good our escape.

"Don't ever do another one of those," Nick said, grabbing the tiller while I hoisted the jib.

Nick: I was worried. During the night's exertions I had felt my hernia pop and now it felt horribly uncomfortable. It's not yet a full blown hernia, just a very thin spot that bulges and that the doctor said was caused by growing too much, too fast. He had claimed that if I took care of it I might get away without it tearing open completely. Right now I was not sure what I'd done, but I didn't want to tell Seb about it.

We're both running on empty, but we're so close to making it that I'd have to be three-quarters dead to stop now. In addition to the hernia, my arms ache, my back aches, my legs ache, my hands and fingers ache, and my neck and whole skull aches. Apart from that I'm fine.

Actually, I'm not. I suffered a tragedy last night. When we lay back and watched the stars after Rocky was safely tied up, I put my hand onto the change pouch in my swimmers, expecting to touch Carla's good luck plastic gem. It had gone. This morning I searched my other pair of swimmers, in case I had made a mistake and it wasn't in the ones I was wearing. Not there either. I had made a solemn vow to myself to keep this bright pink treasure forever and now, in a night of madness, it was lost beneath the waters of Cala Cranc. I was mortified.

Luckily, in my grieving and decrepit state, we had an easy run to Illetas and even sailed around a few islets to waste some time on the way so that the beach wouldn't be too crowded when we arrived.

Seb handed me a piece of rope.

"Let's have a re-run of last night then."

Unbelievably, I was completely unable to tie a bowline! I spent the rest of the trip practicing time and time and time again. Now, finally, it's official. I can tie a bowline in my sleep, and probably while in a deep irreversible coma.

From five o'clock onwards, our friends started trickling onto the sand. Little Alice brought my guitar, which I had been really missing. Big Alice brought her guitar too and all our closest friends arrived with burgers and sausages plus a portable barbecue.

A security guard in a fluorescent jacket kept looking over at us. We could hear him having a tough time with a very grumpy lady whose car had been locked in the car park and who had decided to light a barbecue on the beach while she and her friends waited.

"You can't light a barbecue on this beach," he told her as we swiftly tried to hide ours behind Rocky.

She was giving him a right earful and pointing at us. He began striding towards our group and we braced ourselves for an onslaught.

Our friends joined us on Illetas beach for our last night of the trip.

"OK chicos," he said as he arrived, looking suitably stern before dropping his voice, "you can light your barbecue the minute she goes because she's just being grumpy and rude. But do me a favour and move to the other side of the beach, that's out of my jurisdiction so I can't tell you off for anything over there. Also if you barbecue and put your tents on that little piece of concrete then technically you're not on the beach at all, so you can do whatever you like," he concluded with a bit of impressive finger wagging enacted specifically for the benefit of the watching grumpy lady and her friends.

He also told us to bring Rocky further up the beach – as if we needed reminding after last night! – because there is a strange pressure anomaly here which makes the water come right up the beach at night, which is why the sand is always flat and slightly damp.

He was correct. In fact we left it slightly too late and suddenly water surged around our bags soaking everything. With all our friends around we easily lifted Rocky up to the spot where the pedaloes were stored, while the beach remained underwater all night.

We intended to be true party animals that night. Tomorrow we would be home. By midnight we were dead. We desperately tried to stay up and enjoy the final few hours of our incredibly special journey. A huge half-moon hung directly opposite the middle of the bay, leaving a walkway of silver across the blackened water and up into the sky, but even this beauty couldn't stop our eyelids from drooping. Seb was sitting bolt upright, cross-legged within our circle of friends. He was fast asleep. When he began snoring lightly Little Alice poked him. He groaned, collapsed onto all fours and crawled onto his li-lo. We had been so sure we would see the dawn in, that we hadn't even bothered to pitch the tent. I followed him almost immediately.

Photo by: Jade Lovely

Day Twelve

Nick: We were under strict instructions to arrive at Portixol at one thirty. Most people who wanted to come and welcome us back were able to take a lunch break from work at that time, so we were ordered to be punctual.

Illetas is only a couple of hours' sail away, but we could not stay on the beach once people started arriving in the morning. We spent a few hours sailing round in circles to waste time. During the last twelve days we have noticed how little shade Rocky offers and today we seemed to fry more than ever.

We tried to do some question and answer videos so we could use them to make the power-point presentation MOJOS Marine Help wants us to show at the October boat show in Pollença.

By one twenty our Mums and people on the beach were searching the horizon and seeing absolutely nothing. We are rather small, and we were quite a long way out. Apparently my Mum was getting particularly worried because Gabriel Alomar, from the newspaper Ultima Hora, had arrived to do a follow-up story, and she didn't want to waste his time. She got so worked up she decided to leave the beach crowd and walk along the harbour wall to get a better view.

We'd been sailing around out there for so long. We had our entrance timed perfectly. At one twenty-five we turned onto a broad reach, let out our sails and made a bee-line for the port, executing a perfect jibe to take us straight through the mid-point of the harbour walls.

Looking around to see where all the people were, we could only spy Mum leaping around on top of the wall making expansive hand gestures.

"I reckon she was pretty impressed by that manoeuvre!" I said to Seb as we ploughed on. Seb looked back at his appreciative audience of one.

"Do you think it's possible she's trying to tell us something?"

"Ehhh?" It was a long time for her to be leaping around. We'd done nothing particularly awesome since the jibe. She can be exuberant, but this was a little over the top.

"She's trying to tell us to go to the beach."

"Right you are," Seb said, executing the nautical equivalent of a handbrake turn and screeching back out to sea.

And there they were: Mo and Sebastian from MOJOS, Jay from Kip McGrath, Captain Kevin waving his stick, Simon from The Islander magazine and a host of other friends and family.

The one thing I'm known for among the girls in my class is being a good hugger. Not too long, never awkward, but I do enjoy a good hug, and here was a hugging bonanza! I hugged everyone. People I knew; people I didn't; probably a few random tourists who got caught up in the crowd by mistake, but nobody seemed to mind. It felt so good. So special. But in many ways it didn't hit me that we'd actually completed the trip. It was really emotional, but I didn't believe we'd done it. Not then. We had talked about sailing round the island for so long, and built up to it for so many months, that the concept of it being over didn't hit me for days, and even then there was still SailAid stuff going on.

Once I had finally finished hugging, Captain Kevin came over and gave us two clean, pressed fifty euro notes, so that was one donation we no longer had to chase.

And then everyone was saying their "goodbyes" and we realised we'd have to attempt to leave the beach into the jaws of a fifteen knot wind directly against us. With all the swimmers around, there was no way to do it apart from paddling.

Waves were crashing over the bow and we were paddling like we never had before, but Rocky was making miserable headway.

"This is absolutely bloody ridiculous!" Seb was beginning to vent big time. "If they'd just come to the port and been sensible …"

It was time to get over the side, paddling was making no impression on the distance we had to go and Seb was becoming exceedingly annoyed. I leapt over the side and grabbed the painter. Now the waves were just crashing over my head and I wasn't sure I doing much better than the paddles. Agonisingly slowly we made it into the calm of the harbour water and I flopped back over the side.

"A totally bloody stupid thing to make us do!" I agreed with Seb, and we enjoyed a very thorough vent together. That final paddle and swim ended up being the physically hardest half hour of the entire trip. Finally we made the slipway. We stowed the rudder and centreplate, rolled up the sails, put on her cover, and slung some sopping bags in the back of the car.

"Bye mate," Seb said. "See you soon."

"OK, see you."

And we were going our separate ways. It was over.

I lay in the bath, which was weird in itself in the middle of a Mallorcan July, but the bathroom was quiet.

It felt natural being around the house, with the home comforts all about me again, and yet it was different. I was different.

Usually, when I come home after a couple of days away, I'll go straight out to see my friends. I want to talk and shout with everybody. Now I didn't want to see them at all.

It wasn't just that I was tired, although I'll admit that for the first two days I'd be unconscious if I even thought about a pillow, let alone got horizontal, but apart from that, I just felt weird. Happy weird. But weird all the same.

I needed to think, to remember all the funny times we'd had and the beautiful places we'd seen and the beautiful people we'd met. They were too special to be talked about yet. I needed to savour them, to make sure the scenes and faces were imprinted in my mind forever and I would never forget a single precious moment.

Seb: As we drove away from Rocky it felt magical; the day seemed unreal, yet real at the same time. Mum dropped me at home before having to dash back to work.

I walked into the kitchen and my dog went completely manic. I patted her a bit, but I didn't feel like playing. I felt different, really strange.

I had some cold water and inspected the fridge, then went and lay down in my bedroom for ages thinking about what we'd done and how we'd got on.

I was knackered but there was too much going on in my brain to sleep. It was great to have dinner and all the home amenities again, but I had no wish to get in touch with anyone. The house was familiar but somehow everything was different.

That evening I was shattered, so I went to bed but I couldn't sleep. I spent five hours with my eyes wide open. I was too comfortable. I tried everything; turning the fan on, turning it off, lying on one side and then the other, counting sheep. Nothing worked.

It was bizarre. I'm the person who can sleep absolutely anywhere, even sitting upright, but now I couldn't drop off however hard I tried. I went downstairs and made a sandwich. Lying on the sofa, I finally managed to sleep.

I spent the next two days sitting at home, mainly just thinking and being quiet. Going through everything I'd learnt in my head.

Afterwards

Seb: Although I could have happily remained zombified for at least a week, there was still a lot to do. We had to collect all the money Mediterranea was owed and we had quite a bit of press attention from the Majorca Daily Bulletin, Ultima Hora, Euro Weekly and the sailing magazine Gaceta Nautica. We had also been invited onto Radio One Mallorca.

We were a bit star struck by this invitation as we both remembered Richie Prior, the radio boss, from the amazing acrobatic show, Pirates, which we had seen him in several times when we were taken by the Cubs and Scouts years previously.

Unlike the Talk Radio Europe interview we had done before, this one would be in a studio rather than over the phone. To ensure we both arrived on time, I slept at Nick's the night before so that Steph could take us both in the morning. This proved to be a very bad move.

Little Alice and a group of her friends had been invited to an 80s party the night before so, to get in the mood, they put the full seven disc 80s music collection to play over the car's Parrot system. Just as they'd put the volume up to "Max" the Parrot control batteries died and so there was no way of turning it down, pausing, stopping or doing anything to abate the noise. As this had happened at around midnight, there was nowhere open to buy a new battery and so Steph had driven straight home, battered by sound all the way.

The minute the key turned in the ignition to take us to the radio station we were blasted by "Karma, karma, karma, karma, karma Chameleon ... they come and go, they come and go-o-o-o ..." at massive volume.

For future reference, coffee is a far less effective wake-up method than either watching your boat being swept out to sea, or being subjected to 80s music at intolerable decibels.

To say we arrived in a confused mind set would be an understatement, but we managed to smile and then got totally freaked out when they started fiddling about with electronics and big microphones and earphones.

The reproduction through the earphones was even louder than the 80s music in the car. We really felt persecuted by sound waves and were trying to work out how Richie and Ayesha avoided permanent ear damage, but then they suddenly said "Hi" and we were off.

It was early-ish in the morning, we'd had an unfortunate car ride and we were completely unprepared for any questions that required us to think. Even a little.

"What music do you like?"

"Errrrr"

"Ummmmm"

"Well, what music did you play on the boat?"

We had played a bit of everything, but at that particular millisecond of radio time we couldn't think of the name of even one singer or band.

There was a terrifying amount of "Erring" and "Ummming" until Nick finally almost screamed, "Jack Johnson", in triumph.

At that point, they really should have left the music questions completely. After all, it had taken us five excruciating minutes to come up with one name!

"Who else?"

We were so obviously on a loser! Panicking and stuttering we stumbled through the rest of the interview and were massively relieved to be shown the door. We had really embarrassed ourselves.

Nick: After we returned home we discovered that the swans we had admired in Sa Calobra were escapees and belonged to the town of Andratx. In order to keep them in the municipality their wings had been clipped, but the fab four were hell bent on freedom and so had swum all the way from Andratx port right up the North West coast to end up in the Torrent de Pareis. I was quite sad that the town was insisting on their return, they must have paddled so hard!

We needed to tell people how much we had raised for Mediterranea so Seb's Mum asked Dr. Stoma to let us know how much had been paid into the Mediterranea account under the name of SailAid, and we set about collecting all the other promised donations. The figure to date comes to 4,818 euros after The Foggies golf players upped their sponsorship to an amazing 1,330 euros.

Two of The Foggies – Jeff Yorke and Alan Walker. They were our most generous sponsors. Thanks ☺

While we were on the subject of money, I

decided to calculate how much we'd spent on the trip. It came out at one euro and ninety-five cents. This was on two bottles of cold water. Everything else we had needed we'd been given by all the wonderful people we had met along the way. Many more had supported us by voting for us in the Best of British competition; others by making donations to Mediterranea through their website. Hundreds of people we'd never met had "Liked" us on Facebook and begun following our blog. Others had bent their backs to help us move Rocky; had let us fill our water bottles from their tap; had kept our mobiles functioning by lending us a solar panel; had given us a bed and a warm welcome. We knew, one hundred per cent, with no possibility of doubt whatsoever, that we lived in a place where people of all nationalities and cultures were universally pretty awesome.

There were some whose names we will probably never know, like the crew of the white catamaran that shadowed us off the north coast, but, to all of you we have only one thing to say:

Thank You

Your kindness and enthusiasm gave us a summer we will never forget, and provided us with an experience we will relive in our memories every day of our lives.

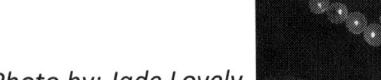

Photo by: Jade Lovely

Thank You ...

AB Victor Segovia Munoz, Abi Saxon Tottman, Adrian Stride, Adro León Rodríguez, Ágata Serrano, Ahmed Abbans, Ahmed Laredj, Aila Bell, Aimee Rebecca Twitchen, Aina Barceló Jordana, Aina Feliu Erica Siri, Aina Ripoll, Ainhoa Rullan Puya, Aitor Poza Román, Alain Gwen'o, Alan Walker, Alan Wilkinson, Alba Vives Membrive, Albert Garcia-Paladini Quetglas, Albert Horrach Pol, Alberto Ferrero, Alejandra Garcia-Salmones Gonzáles, Alejandro Laddaga G, Alex Aviles Fuster, Alex Sanchez Comas, Alex Snufflenpagns Christopherson, Alexis Morrow, Alexnder Lees, Alfonso Sanchez, Ali Rafeek, Alice Page, Alison Jayne Tonge, Amalia Sarmiento Peréz, Aman Sakkrani, Amanda Coleman, Ana García Hernández, Anaïs Estás Que Si, Andrea Blohm, Andreas Nordstrom, Andrew Green, Andy Loynd, Andy Marshall, Angel Kennett-Smith, Angela Twitchen, Angela Williams, Anita Barber, Anna Drzeniek, Anna Pink, Anna Zazo, Anne Sofie Fribo Hjorth, Anne Verrinder, Antón de Llano, Antonia Alorda, Antonia Fluxa Rossello, Antonia Lamballe, Antonio Cerdá Sestrús, Antonio Mateus , Antonius Cramer, Antony Rivolta, Anu Bajpai, Arantxa Ruiz, Aunarella Rando, Axel Verdier Varamo, Aya Carr, Ayesha, Barbara Jago, Bazil Lawrenson, Becky Martin, Becky Morgan, Belen Barea, Belen Sans Cañada, Belinda Shaw, Ben Cooke, Benjamin Shorten, Bernado Lopez Cintrano, Beth Martin, Bishop Beany Butler, Blanca Sebastián, Boating-In Mallorca, Borja Alvarez Martin, Britta Krebs,

Bruno Valderas Cristobal, Callum Stuart Kennedy, Calvia Pet-Vet, Cami Stewart, Candela Baena Vega, Candice Wilkinson, Canon Jim Hawthorne MBE, Captain Kevin O'Regan, Carlos Garavi, Carlos Olmedo, Carlotta Emanuella Nutella a Gazzola, Carmel Dutra, Carmen Valdivieso, Carol Bloom, Carolina Heslam Moreno, Caroline Coffey, Catalina Balle Borrars, Roccardo Giglioli, Cataline Garcia-German, Cati Pons Morey, Charles Varcoe, Charlie McGuigen Rivers-Bland, Charlotte Mott, Charmaine Lawrenson, Chetana Annette, Chris Hudson, Christian Ahler, Christine Vageler, Christopher Mason, Claudia Díaz de Luna, Clive Davies, Cristianiyo Cartagera, Cristina Hernández Blanes, Palma Karol's Land, Dani Ferra Abril , Dani Stoma, Dani Vigo, Daniela Adolfina, Daniela Vidal, Danniel Mulet, Danny Brooks-Franklin, Dave Bladon, David Barlow, David Casado Moreno, David Cole, David Diley, David Ireland, David Moore, Dawne Archer, Dax Allen Vian, Debra Gleeson, Diana Bradley, Diego Fernando Aldas Loor, Diego Maggi, Dina Rosenmeier, Don José Got, Dorothée Bénéteau, Edu Cabot, Eisha Bajpai, Elana Danker Albert, Elena Alberti, Elena Flaquer Massanet, Elena Gomez, Elena Palafuteva, Elisabeth Rigo Andrews, Elizabeth Fre, Ellie O'Donnell, Elodie Behravan, Emily Fill, Emma de Sonsa, End Endrinilla, English Radio Pollensa, Enya Bosch Fernández, Erica Siri, Ernest Navarro, Eugenia Cusi Costa, Eun Young Yoon, Eva Eiroa, Eva Michelena Font, Evelyn Hobbs, Fabia Hohne, Farmacia Guix, Faye Price, Fiona Mccourt, Fiona Rorke Christensen, Fiona Velosa, Florian Gander,

Francesc Baiget Monserrat, Francesca Aras Tardito, François Aov, Franzi Tesche Rebenaque, Frederikke Ahler, Gabriel Alomar, Garreth Jones, Georgia Monaghan, Georgiana Bandac, Gina Nita Rose Mcfarlane, Giovanna Verussa, Gloria Rodriguez Martin, Glynis German, Gonzalo Mendez Blasco, Graeme Ellis, Greyan Bradley, Guille Hard Core, Hannah Biggs, Hannah Gale Tascon, Harry Abbott, Helen Comben, Helen Porter, Helen Warren, Hélène Grangé, Heros Ottaviano, Hicham Chairi, Holy Evans, Hugo Ramon, Huw Richard, India Gibson, Ines Vilajoana, Ir Ma, Irene Figuerola, Isabella Rose Woolger, Isabella So Devine, Ismael Escudero Masa, Ismael Pinto, Ivan Nikolov, Izzy Abad, Izzy Newman, Izzy Richardson, J De Large Oi, Jack Bryant, Jackie Evans, Jackie Lancaster, Jacob Rutherford, Jacqueline Del Rio, Jade Halkier, Jade Lovely, Jaime Garcia Soriano, Jaime Gonzalo, Jake Theander, James B Rieley, James Martin, Jan Siegl, Jane Rolfe, Jane Thompson, Janice Van Brabant, Jason Edmunds, Jaume Ensenyat, Javi Reus Gonzalez, Javier Poncela, Javier Ricón, Jay Hirons, Jazmin Redaelli Cisneros, Jeanne Murphy, Jenny White, Jeroen Meier Mattern, Jessica Yenilmez, Jesus Noguera Salafranca, Jill Witkamp, Jim Bell, Jimena García Germán, Jo Clayton Walsh, Jo Herriot, Jo Orgill, Jo Walton, Joan Balle, Joan James Russon Saez, Joana Clar Ayarte, Joana Maria Llambias Salva, Joanna Young, Joanne Coey, Joaquim Borras, Joe and Maureen Fiteni, Joke Nesbitt-Hawes, Jon Comben, Jonathan Martin Brennan, Jonno Harris, Jonny Ault, Jono Hirons, Jordan Lewis Hodge, Jordi Fernández, Jordi

Muñoz, Jose Miguel Lopez Ibares, Josep Ferrer, Josep Oliver, Josep Vanrell Negre, Joshie Williams, Joshua Munday, Jota Mrtnz, Journal De Bord Gourmand, Joy Brown, Juan Carlos Almazan Olivo, Juan Fernández González, Juan Miguel Galindo Lladó, Juan Valentín Lozano Arnica, Juana Alcover Bibiloni, Juanan Pujals Echavarria, Judith and Niall O'Connor, Judith Ray, Julian Kerp, Julie and Martin Staley, Julie Franklin, Juliette Grice, June Pastor, Justine Knox, Kamil Tomecki, Karen Burke, Katrin Gebhardt, Kay Halley, Ken Williams, Kenneth Franklin, Kenneth Schytte, Kevin Keenan, Kevin Mcdonnell, Kevin O Regan, Kip McGrath Mallorca, Kirsty Winter, KJ Elsdon, Krista Hyer, Laetitia Rocca, Lara Sua, Laura Najera Vallejo, Laura Romero, Laura Ryan, Laura Stadler, Leah Goldsworthy, Lesley Segui, Leticia Van Allen, Levana Bellydance, Linda Spratt, Linda Walker, Lisa Davis, Lisa Keenan, Lois Ana O'Connor Foster, Lorraine Taylor, Loudes Rodríguez González, Louise Balfour, Louise Davis, Lucas Sanchez, Lucía Fidani, Lucia Villajoana, Lucy Bradley, Lucy Jennifer Horner, Lynda Thompson-Spack, Magdalena Arbona Ensenyat, Mai Milos, Majorca Daily Bulletin, Malcolm Jones, Mallorca Days Out, Mallorcasolutions Becky, Mandy Tyrrel, Manolo Cabello Galan, Manuel Casado Rodrigo, Manuel Martinez Iniesta, Manuel Steiner, Mar Folch, Mar Reynes Bestard, Marc Berenguer Chicharito, Marc Ferrá, Marco Kuehn, Marcos Rivero Collado, Mare Ferrá, Marga Serramo Egia, Margaret and Tony Whittaker, Maria Concepción Diaz-Llanos, Maria Cristina Villalobos, Maria Dubois Chicharro, Maria Grimes, Maria Rosa

Gridica Bozzini, Maria S. Koenig-Caple, Maria Smith, Maribel Espallardo, Marina Cardona Rigo, Marina Live, Marina Moll Fontanals, Marina Nausía Bonet, Marina Rodriguez Mari, Mario Diego Ibargüen, Marita, Marjory Jones, Marlis and Hans Juergen Blohm, Marta Alberti, Martin Kircher, Mary and Bob Mason, Matilde Tessa Christensen, Matt White, Maureen Hemingway McLeod, May Riudavets Taura, Mediterranea Ong Ngo, Megan Richter, Melanie Lovely, Melanie Reddington, Melanie Winters, Melody Ellmauer Perez, Merca Nautic, Meritxell Ribas Puigmal, Mia Ensenyat, Mia Guadiola Salvà, Michael Dellar, Michael Stoma, Michelle Bondulich, Mick Sakkal, Miguel Angel Cabañero Capo, Miguel Garcia Reus, Miguel Ricci, Miguel Rubio Ramos, Miguel Salord, Mike Glastone, Mila Una, Miles Wakefield, Milika Aidasani, Miss Pennington, MOJOS Marine Help, Montse Hdez, Montse Tevar Tebé, Mood Beach, Nancy Silvera, Natacha Cozar, Natalia García Coll, Nathalie Lapping, Nautica GDR, Néstor Diego Revuelta, Neus Caldentey, Neus Segura, Nichola Tennant Brown, Nick Frembgen, Nicky & Roger Horner, Nicky Stixx, Nicola Kay, Nicola Tennant Brown, Nofre Segura, Nuna Mari Personat, Nuria Aljam Contreras, Octavian Jalba-Verseck, Oil Guennoun, Olga Duran Mounier, Oli Abbott, Oliver Neilson, Olivia May Green, Olivier Diquero, Ollie Broadley, Omayma El Yaakonbi, Oscar Siches, Oscar Stauffer, Ouig White, P&G Yachting, Paco Segura, Pat Ferguson, Pat Shoreland, Patricia Alehandra Villalobus, Patricia Clar Ramírez, Patricia Gonzalez Baldino, Patricia Nicolau, Pau Lozano, Pau Pomar

Rendon, Paul Davis, Paul Innes, Paula Castellano, Paula Gomila Sbert, Paula Pena Lanzón, Paula Socies Mayol, Pedro Prieto, Pedro Quiroga Troncoso, Pep Miquel Paris Clar, Pere Amer Martí, Peter Tibbs, Phil Marshal, Phil Wolff, Pilates Valeria Mazzola, Plural Salud Ciencias Arte, Rafa Bujosa, Raimon Martínez Mussons, Rebecca Woolger, Renee Nijs, Rhoanna Jackson, Richard Ascough, Richie Prior, Ricky Tollenaere, Rob Salisbury, Robert Mason, Robyn Charleston, Roddy Calo, Roger Swain, Rosa Maria Miguel Moreira, Rosa Veik Laime, Rosie Williams, Rudolf Michael Meis, Sahil Dadlani, Sam Abbott, Sam Brooks, Sam Holland, Sam Thompson, Samantha Louise Barcroft Jones, Sandra Llull, Sandra Moreno, Sara Sánchez, Sarah Drane, Sarah Hardy, Sarah McGrath, Seb Green, Sebastian Danthez, Sebastian Espinosa Espinosa, Serena Socias, Sergio Sastre Aguilar, Sharon Pierce, Sharon Syrett, Sheila Franklin, Sheila Richards, Shelagh Dillon, Shyvone Mhari Blom, Silke Bommersheim, Simon Darnborough, Simon Relph, Sofia Bauza, Sofia Charlotte Green, Son Amar, Sonia Lebron Moreno, Sophia Gaede, Soraya El Boytaybi, Specsavers Santa Ponsa, Stefanie Milla, Stephanie Glover, Steve Andrews, Sue and Alan Wilkinson, Susan Turner, Susana Nadal, Susie Hall, Suzanne Lampard, Talk of the North, Tamia Tiefel, Tammy Mounier, Tatiana, Tayrne Butler, Teo at Palma Media, Teresa Diaz Merlo, Teresa Nicolau, Terry and Nina Franklin, Terry Mott, The Foggies Golf Society, The Islander magazine, Thilan Karunasekera, Thomas Froment, Thomas Schepens Stevens, Tina Jarrett, Tito Fer Ortega, Tom Rohde Pearce, Tomás

Ripoll, Tomeu Mascó, Tommy and Andrea Blohm, Tomy de la Villa, Toni Catala, Toni Perez, Toni Tió Sauleda, Tonina Taracon Melià, Tor Cooper-Evans, Tracy Lambert, Tripti Aidasani, Tristan Kirk Smith, Ultima Hora, Valen Diez, Vanesa Bedoya, Velas Ferrà, Vanessa Martinez, Vicki McLeod, Victor Gaminde Carreras, Victoria de Castro, Victoria Guillen Marti, Violette Salas, Vishal Soomaney, Wendy Sweeney, Will Lewis, Will Scott, Xisco and Jose Miguel, Xisco Salva Rossich, Zara Dickerson, Zoila María Checa Molina

Huge apologies to anyone whose name we may have missed. If you let us know via Facebook who you are, we'll update future copies in paperback and on Kindle.

If you have any questions about the trip or would like to see all the photos in the book in high resolution colour then please get in touch with us via:

www.facebook.com/two.boys.in.a.boat

If you enjoyed reading Two Boys and a Boat it would be **awesome** if you could leave a small review – or a big one if you prefer! – on amazon.co.uk or amazon.com.

Your Amazon reviews and "Likes" on Facebook are incredibly important to us and make us know there are even more Very Nice People out there. **Thank you.**

Nick Mason and Sebastian Page Franklin

Made in the USA
San Bernardino, CA
21 April 2016